BROKEN
unto
WHOLENESS

Wounded Soldiers Marching toward Victory

MARILYN HANSEN

ISBN 978-1-0980-1834-4 (paperback)
ISBN 978-1-0980-1835-1 (digital)

Christian Faith Publishing, Inc.
832 Park Avenue
Meadville, PA 16335
www.christianfaithpublishing.com

Printed in the United States of America

To my dear husband Gary, whom God has used as an instrument of encouragement and affirmation throughout our fifty-five years of marriage. God is my Source, and he has used my dear husband Gary, as my source here on earth to assist me in being obedient to His call to write *Broken unto Wholeness* for His honor and glory.

WORDS OF COMMENDATION

Marilyn Hansen is not the first to plead, "Cast me not away from your presence and take not your Holy Spirit from me. Restore to me the joy of your salvation and uphold me with a willing spirit" (Psalm 51:11–12). Nor is she the first to seek to be "strengthened with power through His Spirit in (my) inner being" (Ephesians 3:16). She will not be ignored by her heavenly Father or be left alone to bandage her own wounds.

As you read *Broken unto Wholeness*, you will understand why she desires to crawl into the trenches carrying God's healing to others while not yet fully whole herself.

It is not news that someone is broken. Marilyn desires to share Good News that Broken unto Wholeness is a Kingdom Plan.

—Dean Benton
Spiritual Father, Pastor,
Evangelist, Author

Above all else, Marilyn has been driven by her hunger to be healed of her own broken soul and to be used by God to loosen the chains of injustice, break the yoke to set the oppressed free, and to instill hope in Jesus (Isaiah 58:6).

Through the years of our deep friendship, my friend Marilyn has sought those who could help untie her cords of depression and help her find the causes of her brokenness. She found quality and significant professionals, friends, and pastors who carefully tended her wounds. Each one brought hope and blessed her for ministry. They brought hope for wholeness. In *Broken unto Wholeness*, Marilyn shares her journey to being a woman of God still being healed. Her desire is to love others hungry to be healed.

—Carole Benton
Spiritual Mother, Pastor's wife,
Teacher, Author

Marilyn's striking metaphors, vivid descriptions, and probing questions give confident answers to our quest for wholeness, even in the pain of a fallen, broken world where all of us are broken people.

All of these are part of Marilyn's autobiographical/devotional book, *Broken unto Wholeness*, which effectively challenges us to give ourselves completely to the One Who takes our brokenness and remolds pieces of our lives to bring wholeness. This process continues as we march toward wholeness, victory, and heaven.

—Yvonne Moulton
Retired Professor of English
Asbury University

Broken unto Wholeness: Wounded Soldiers Marching toward Victory is a book that every believer and unbeliever should read to realize that each of us goes through difficult and sometimes seemingly overwhelming experiences. Yet if we allow Him, God is ever-present to help us through them with a redemptive result for us and those around us. This book is powerful, sometimes difficult to read, challenging, and, most of all, encouraging. I have known Marilyn for many years and have been aware of many of the experiences mentioned in her book. I can attest to her complete and continual trust in God for His will in her life. I encourage you to go on this journey of trials and tribulations and the march toward victory.

—Wade Zachary
Pastor, Professor, Chaplain,
Counselor

CONTENTS

FOREWORD

God likes to display His glory. The created universe shows His power and majesty. But the beauty of His holiness and the infinite reaches of His love comes through most clearly in people who are endowed with a mind to know Him. Our first parents were deceived by Satan and decided to go their own way, thereby bringing death upon the human race.

The rebellion of mankind did not change God's love, and in the fullness of time, God came in the person of Jesus to bear the judgment of our sin so that we could become a new creation in Christ. However, redemption does not deliver us from the realities of a weak body, physical limitations, and hurtful, damaging experiences.

There will be many adversities because we live in a fallen world. So it is not surprising that the Christian life involves struggles and overcoming disappointments. God works through our weakness and failures to make us dependent upon His grace every day.

Marilyn Hansen has gathered in this book real life stories, poems, testimony, and Scriptures that will inspire and uplift the soul. Her deep compassion for persons who have gone through trials is evident in these pages. Giving authenticity to the account is the author's own experience of brokenness and overcoming many difficulties through the grace of a loving Savior. Nothing here is theoretical. She analyzes the emotions that accompany suffering and applies scriptural principles for obtaining freedom from damaged emotions. The truth is that all of us are wounded in different ways and continually need to realize the infinite resources of divine grace.

Growing through pain is a choice. Her honest and insightful reflections provide practical guidance toward becoming the person God has designed us to be. God is not finished with any of us yet.

The author's insights and wise advice challenges us that we do not have to stay wounded but can experience victory in Christ.

Dr. Robert E. Coleman

Distinguished Professor of Evangelism and Discipleship Emeritus,

Lecturer, and Mentor

Note: Dr. Coleman has authored several books, including *Master Plan of Evangelism.*

APPRECIATION

To my heavenly Father God, for calling me to be His child and servant in the Name of His Son Jesus, and Who is my source for living and writing *Broken unto Wholeness*, and to Whom I give all the glory!

To my Savior and Lord Jesus Christ, for dying for my sins and making me *broken unto wholeness*.

To the Holy Spirit, Who is my helper and Who gave me utterance as I wrote *Broken unto Wholeness*.

To my parents Gene and Mabel Sturgeon, who God chose for me to be their child when He created me.

To my beloved husband Gary, who has been my source of love, support, affirmation, and encouragement for over five decades.

To my beautiful daughter Michelle, for her love and for being my prayer partner on my journey of writing *Broken unto Wholeness*.

To my son Greg, for being *worried sick* as I traversed serious illness, and his willingness to take my place if he could.

To my brother Ron, for the privilege of leading him into a personal relationship with Jesus. And to his wife Sandy, with whom we have laughed together, cried together, and supported each other on our personal journeys.

To my father, who has gone on to meet his Maker, for the privilege of introducing him to his Savior, Jesus.

To my spiritual parents Dean and Carole Benton, who God used to lead me into a personal relationship with Jesus and who continue to plant seeds.

To Pastor William Johnson, who held my hand as I walked through the valley of the shadow of death.

To Mentor Dorene Rentz, who God used on my journey of being made *broken unto wholeness.*

To Doctor William Simons, who God used to rekindle hope in my life when I had lost all hope.

To Doctor Mitchael Estridge, who God used to illumine things in my past that were still haunting me.

To Pastor and friend Wade Zachary—Just Wade—for being my friend and for caring for me as we shared our journeys and laughed together.

To my dear friend Allen, who made an investment in my life and for giving me a laptop computer to write *Broken unto Wholeness.*

To friend Rick, for giving me a large-key keyboard so I could type *Broken unto Wholeness* with one finger easier. And also for founding a hair foundation in my honor for home-bound people in the Lexington area.

To hairstylist Lois, for coming to our home to do my hair and that of numerous other home-bound people in the area.

To my dear friend Sarah Dunn, who loved, supported, and encouraged me to reach out with the gifts God endowed. She shall always remain in my heart!

To my dear friend Joyce Blevens, for her friendship and encouragement to write *Broken unto Wholeness,* her positive attitude in the face of adversity, and her smile that will live in my heart always!

To friend Dr. Robert E. Coleman, for inspiration in writing *Broken unto Wholeness.*

To Arhia, age seven; Rhian, age eight; and Clem, ninety, for their prayer support in writing *Broken unto Wholeness,* along with friends Shirley, ninety-two; Robbie, eighty-eight; Yvonne, eighty-two; and every age in between.

To Courtney and Meghan Roberts, for their friendship and prayer support in writing *Broken unto Wholeness.*

To my Asheville Care Group, for their friendship and caring.

To my Lexington Life Group, for their prayer support in writing *Broken unto Wholeness.*

To my family and friends, who have prayed for me throughout writing *Broken unto Wholeness*. You will always hold a special place in my heart.

I shall be indebted for eternity to all of these loved ones for their unique touch on my life and for being part of God's plan to mold me into His person and the likeness of His Son by making me *Broken unto Wholeness*.

MY COMMISSION

God called me and equipped me to proclaim the Good News of Jesus Christ that He might set His captives free through me. I go forth in His power for His Glory!

MY STORY

"You saw me before I was born and scheduled each day of my life before I began to breathe. Every day was recorded in your book" (Psalm 139:16).

THE BEGINNING

The Word Became Flesh

"In the beginning was the Word, and the Word was with God, and the Word was God. He was with God in the beginning. Through Him all things were made; without Him nothing was made that has been made. In Him was life, and that life was the light of all mankind. The light shines in the darkness, and the darkness has not understood it" (John 1:1–5).

"He was in the world, and though the world was made through Him, the world did not recognize Him. He came to that which was His own, but His own did not receive Him. Yet to all who did receive Him, to those who believed in His Name, He gave the right to become children of God" (John 1:10–12).

"The Word became flesh and made His dwelling among us. We have seen His glory, the glory of the One and Only Son, who came from the Father, full of grace and truth" (John 1:14).

> Every life has a story.
> Every story has a lesson.
> And every story deserves to be told.
> You are in charge of your own book.
>
> —Oprah Winfrey

It is my prayer that God will fill my writings with the breathings of His Spirit to yours, as you read its pages. A DaySpring card reads: "God is writing a book about *you*. The pages tell of your life and the lives *you* were created to touch. No one else will take exactly the same path as *you*, meet the same people, or have a chance to show the love of God in the same way. *You* are unique and so is your story…and it's one of the Author's favorite reads." I pray the next chapter holds more good things than you can imagine.

"I think sometimes we rush the narrative construction of our seasons. We are eager to wring the lesson and the hope and the story out of our lives in order to make sense of them. We are ready to move on! But sometimes the story isn't clear until we've lived a few more chapters. Time reveals what was really going on, and there is no shortcut for an unfolding life. Sometimes the full story won't be clear to us until years have passed and then we see the hand of God, or we see old things with new eyes. This is grace." (Sarah Bessely)

Roy Lessin writes, "God delights in turning the pages of our lives so that He can write exciting new chapters."

Every one of us has a story to share. I pray that my story will leave an imprint on your life and on our relationship. You are important to God, and you are important to me! May the Holy Spirit add His blessing to my sharing. Appreciating you as we journey together, as He makes all of us…

Broken unto Wholeness.

THE SEARCH

> Have mercy on me, O God, according to Your unfailing love; according to Your great compassion blot out my transgressions. Wash away all my iniquity and cleanse me from my sin. (Psalm 51:1–2)

Do you feel broken, split or cracked into pieces, splintered, fractured, not functioning properly, violated, beaten, or bankrupt? Are you tired of feeling broken, torn up, pulled apart, raped, bruised, and void of the energy and resources to make your life functional—worth living? My friend, the Creator of mankind stands ready to make the fragmented pieces of your life whole in Jesus' Name.

> Create in me a pure heart, O God, and renew a steadfast spirit within me. Do not cast me from Your presence or take Your Holy Spirit from me. Restore to me the joy of Your salvation and grant me a willing spirit, to sustain me. (Psalm 51:10–12)

The Christ, who was bruised and broken on Mount Calvary on Good Friday, was raised to new life Easter morn. We can experience that kind of resurrection in our lives as well. He longs to raise us to new heights with Him and give our lives purpose and meaning for living. Wholeness comes only through intentional, intimate, ongoing communion with the living Christ. Commune with Him and experience His resurrection power in your life. "May God Himself, the God of peace, sanctify you through and through. May your whole spirit, soul, and body be kept blameless at the coming of our Lord

Jesus Christ. The One who calls you is faithful, and He will do it" (1 Thessalonians 5:23–24).

> The sacrifices of God are a broken spirit; a broken
> and contrite heart, O God, You will not despise.
> (Psalm 51:17)

Is your spirit broken? Is your heart contrite? Then the God of compassion stands ready to forgive you. He awaits you with open arms. He does not look down upon you, but rather, it is His desire to lift you up and set you on a path of righteousness for not only your sake but also His. He sacrificed His only Son to die for your brokenness. Don't let His death be in vain on your behalf. Let Him embrace you, give you a holy kiss, and make you whole in Jesus' Name.

In the next chapter, I will share my personal testimony about how "I overcame by the blood of the Lamb and by the word of my testimony" (Revelation 12:11). May the words of my mouth and meditations of my heart, glorify the God and Father of our Lord Jesus Christ by His Holy Spirit.

Won't you join me on this journey as we explore avenues of healing, which come not in the questions or in the answers, but in *The Search.*

MY TESTIMONY

Never will I leave you; never will I forsake you.
(Hebrews 13:5)

I was born in central Iowa and grew up on a farm with a sibling, Donna, seventeen months older than myself. Later, two sisters and a brother—five, seven, and nine years younger—joined our family. I don't recall a lot of my early childhood. My parents both worked very hard, and I commend them for their commitment to the American dream and their integrity in striving to meet their goals. However, they each had their story and carried their own knapsack of unfulfilled dreams and failed expectations. It behooves those of us who have been made *broken unto wholeness*, to reach out with the love of our Lord and make a difference in lives torn apart by countless pangs of shattered dreams and broken promises.

I was in my tenth year when heartbreak settled on our household—a hot August day when tragedy struck like lightening. Donna and I had had a childish quarrel over sharing some candy when my mother left to drive her into town for a piano lesson. A mile and a half down our dusty gravel road, a tractor—pulling a hay baler with a load of hay—came up a rise in the middle of the road toward our homestead in Iowa. My mother swerved to miss it, but it crushed the passenger side of the car where Donna was sitting. Mom was critically injured and blamed herself for the accident, though it wasn't her fault. Within a flash, my family was inalterably changed.

The two and a half agonizing weeks Donna lay unconscious, I rode my bicycle round and around our farmyard—looking toward the heavens—asking Someone up there to save her life so I could tell her I was sorry about our quarrel and ask her forgiveness. However, much to my dismay, she did not survive the accident, abandoning me with two decades of guilt and remorse. I would carry the secret burden of guilt on my subconscious level that weighed on my spirit like an albatross around my neck for twenty years before accepting Jesus as my Savior.

My mother was driving the car which precipitated her own woundedness for the remainder of her days on this earth. In fact, she confessed to her pastor—in her last fleeting moments—that she was afraid to die, lest Donna still be angry with her. Torment had stalked her most of her adult life until she drew her last breath.

I accepted Jesus as my personal Lord and Savior on November 8, 1972. My first year as a child of God was a supernatural Damascus Road experience. My beloved husband Gary, saw such a transformation in my life that he asked Jesus into his heart two months later, and our five-year-old daughter Michelle, two months after her daddy. And the Holy Spirit used me to lead several friends into His saving grace—whom I look forward to spending eternity with.

But almost exactly a year into my spiritual journey of traversing the mountain tops with my Lord, I suffered a severe depression—not wanting to live—spending five days in a psychiatric ward just days before Christmas with two small children. The hardest part of that despairingly painful time was feeling separated from my new special friend, Jesus—the One Who listened to the lonely cry of my heart, wiped my tears with the hem of His garment, and encircled my burdened shoulders with His gentle Spirit. The smothering pain felt like it could snuff out my very breath as I gasped to be set free from its clutches. How I longed for His tender compassion with every fiber of my being!

By sheer grace from on high, my two young children survived this desert time, while I felt parched by the isolation of sojourners to accompany me on this frightening, desolate pilgrimage. I attributed my survival to the support of my loving, consoling husband and the counsel of a godly pastor/psychologist, who took hold of my hand and started me on the path toward wholeness. Pastor Johnson helped me understand and deal with the guilt that had riddled my psyche and tormented my spirit beyond comprehension.

After months of holding fast to the Savior of my soul, Who, though I didn't sense His presence, was leading me on my journey toward wholeness. I asked Him one day, "What was my depression about? What are you trying to teach me?" And in my spirit, He replied clearly, with great understanding on His part and mine, "I allowed you to be broken to make you whole." Over forty-five years later, He is still leading me down the path that is making me *broken unto wholeness.* Hence, His call on my life to write this book.

I am embarrassed to confess that I still struggle with guilt that robbed me of the joy of living much of my adult life. But much to my delight, God has not only used that most sorrowful experience to put me on a path toward healing, but also I have been able to minister to other wounded souls and witness them come into their personal healing. I have found no greater fulfillment in life than to be used by my Lord to bring other wounded souls into a personal relationship with Him and into His healing presence.

Over the years, I have learned there are different levels of healing as there are different levels of a mountain, but each is just as important as another. We can't climb to the top of a mountain in one stride and, more often than not, God brings us into wholeness one step at a time. If we try to bypass a particular level, our healing might not be as complete. If mountains were smooth, we couldn't climb them.

I have also learned that when we experience pain in our lives, God can use our woundedness to minister to others and bring them on the healing journey, as well. As we yield to Him and allow Him to work His divine plan in our lives, He is able to fulfill His plan. Romans 8:28 tells us, "We know that in *all* things, He works for the good of those who love Him, who have been called according to His purpose." And allowing Him to use our suffering for His glory is what makes it victorious for Him and for us.

Are you able to nail your brokenness to the foot of His cross or are you unwilling to let loose of it and allow Him to make you *broken unto wholeness?* Sometimes we choose to remain in prisons without bars—even prisons of our own making. Is it your desire to be held captive by your self-imposed imprisonment or would you like to be set free from the chains that bind you?

Verse one of Isaiah 61 tells us, "He has sent me to bind up the brokenhearted, to proclaim freedom for the captives and release from darkness for the prisoners." And First Peter 2:24 (NKJV) says, "He Himself bore our sins in His body on the tree, so that we might die to sins and live for righteousness; by His wounds you have been healed."

Jesus came to bind up your wounds and make you whole in His Name. He is waiting to bestow His healing touch on your life. He died for your woundedness. Don't let Him have died in vain while you live in pain. Choose to let Him make you *broken unto wholeness*.

Several years ago, I believe God spoke to my spirit about writing a book entitled *Broken unto Wholeness*. My subtitle is *Wounded Soldiers Marching toward Victory*. "Oh, dear God, please help me be obedient to Your call on my life that I might bring honor and glory to You who blesses all Your children with Your presence and loving-kindness."

So I am grateful for these events that brought me to a place of not only *hope* but also *insight* for a future bright with joy unspeakable and full of glory. God is good beyond measure and faithful to His Word.

Thus, God is our only hope of redemption from guilt and its snares that bind us. And it is His desire that we be set free from this albatross that weighs on us until we are stooped with remorse and self-loathing. Even though our lives will never be problem-free, we need to cut the tie that binds us so we can move forward, unencumbered by feelings of blame and shame. We need to let God make us...

Broken unto Wholeness.

FAMILY BURIAL GROUND

Our Lord tells us:
Peace I leave with you; My peace I give you.
I do not give to you as the world gives.
Do not let your hearts be troubled and do not
    be afraid.
(John 14:27)

We have all seen cemeteries with tombstones erected next to churches. How many secrets lie beneath the ground—never to be revealed—marked with untold bygone sins? How many hidden family mysteries have yet to be told? That families live disconnected from one another should be of no surprise to any of us. We all have tendencies to hide behind a shroud of hidden motives and untold agendas. We need to ask ourselves: "Where is God in all of this?" Do we have the courage to fess up to Him? He already knows those things that cause us to wither from the truth that lies within.

My family is currently on such a pilgrimage. The wreckage of an accident that occurred sixty-five years ago is sprouting up out of its burial ground and rearing its ugliness, robbing my mother of peace on her journey to her resting place. How can a human soul live with such pain and torment throughout their entire adult life? How can she bear the scars of an accident that was not her fault? How can she have been blamed for decades for something that ripped at her heart daily? How can others hold her guilty when guilt has been her constant companion? With Jeremiah, her parched lips cry out, "They dress my wounds as if they were not serious. Peace, peace they say, when there is no peace" (8:11).

Guilt robs us of the joy of living. It eats at our innermost being until we are devoid of that which gives us joy and hope for our future.

How can we live with our accusers while they point their fingers and stare us in the face for our mistakes? Life becomes shallow with those things that tear at our emotions and torture our spirits.

Jesus came to heal the brokenhearted. So why do we refuse to allow Him to become our refuge? Somehow we find comfort in beating ourselves at the whipping post of life—until our lives become fleeting—and we can no longer cope with that which eats our lunch, causing ulcers in the process.

Christians are supposed to be healing agents to those God brings across our path. How can our mother have born such deep-rooted pain throughout her life and never shared the ache in her heart? How can loved ones push away those who long to be healed and made whole? Does the grave beckon them from their misery? How many corpses are crying out for peace they never knew while alive? Are they ready to meet their Maker? Are we ready to let them meet the Master?

God has a plan for each of our lives. He came to give us hope and a future (Jeremiah 29:11). It is His desire that we live in the peace that He is. He longs for His peace to be shed abroad in our hearts.

What residue is passed on to those she bore? How does that same pain implanted in their lives become destructive and life-altering for them? How do they pick up the pieces of this fragmented puzzle and let the peace of Christ rule in their hearts? The responsibility does not lie at her doorstep. We must each take responsibility for our own lives. We must allow God to make us *broken unto wholeness.*

The wages of sin is death—not her sin but ours. Christ came to set us free from the wages of sin. We must release those things that have bound us and held us captive for most of our lives. Let us release those things that bind us and not take them to our graves. Then our epitaph shall read, "And the peace of God, which transcends all understanding, will guard your hearts and your minds in Christ Jesus" (Philippians 4:7).

Mother died on November 27, 2007.

MISS ME—BUT LET ME GO

When I come to the end of the road
And the sun has set for me,
I want no rites in a gloom-filled room,
Why cry for a soul set free?

Miss me a little—but not for long,
And not with your head bowed low.
Remember the love that was once shared,
Miss me—but let me go.

For this is a journey we all must take
And each must go alone.
It's all part of the Master's plan
A step on the road to home.

When you are lonely and sick of heart,
Go to the friends we know.
And bury your sorrows in doing good deeds…
Miss me—but let me go.

Mother's funeral service, November 30, 2007

GONE BUT NOT FORGOTTEN

Friend, o Friend,
So many hearts feel sad.
My heart grieves for you,
And the pain you carried in yours.
After being memorialized by family and friends,
You are interred with saints gone before.
Some tombstones are simple, others elaborate,
Some with just a marker, others' their names etched on a rock.
Some decorated with flowers,
Others are scars from previous wars.
Some carry spiritual titles: Reverend and Deacon,
While others are nameless without reason.
One bore this year of our Lord,
Others are weathered beyond recognition.
Some were born in another century,
Others went before their time.
Friend, o Friend, your passing came too soon.
Rest, dear one, in Jesus' arms.
We are standing on holy ground,
As we await the trumpet sound.
We'll greet you in the air one day,
And commune in heaven to stay.
From this earth, you are:
Gone but not forgotten.

November 30, 2004

GUILT

Therefore, there is now no condemnation for those who are in Christ Jesus. (Romans 8:1)

Guilt is an emotion that can wreak havoc on our well-being and ravage our very souls. It can eat our lunch and cause indigestion that can last a lifetime. It is born out of feelings that can be misunderstood, misconstrued, or mistaken for things we imagine to be true but, in reality, are lies we allow to permeate our thoughts over which we have no control.

As I shared in my testimony, I have been riddled with guilt for over six decades, robbing me of my joy of living. The seed was planted when my sister Donna, was killed in a car accident. We had had a childish quarrel over candy when I was ten years old. My mother was taking her into town for a piano lesson when a tractor came over a rise in the middle of the gravel road just down from the farm I grew up on in Iowa. It struck the car where my sister was sitting and—in a solitary moment—my selfishness erupted like a volcano, spewing molten ash over those who crossed my path. I would carry the residue of my actions the rest of my life.

How does a child cope with an emotion that pervades their innocence and robs them of enjoying their childhood—perhaps their adulthood—and possibly until they draw their last breath? Guilt can be a culprit that locks us in a prison from which we cannot escape. The bars become vices that lock us into a cell of self-contempt and even into the cells of our very existence.

Does guilt hang around your neck like an albatross? Are there times when the weight of it feels as if it could break your spirit? Do you wish you could bury it in a sea of forgetfulness? I feel your burden, my friend.

How do we overcome the aftermath of things we have done when our very being has been shaken to the core and lies in ruins? Who do we trust with our deepest secrets when betrayal could haunt us until eternity? How do we let go of that which has been bred in our souls? How can we come from being made *broken unto wholeness?*

As much as we would like, we can't abort the truth. Truth is the fiber of what we believe. We must go forward—as a ship being steered by its rudder—while avoiding the seaweed that entangles us. Somehow, we must break free from those things that would pull us down into the depths.

Has the serpent of guilt ever slithered under the back door of your soul? It can be like a snake that clutches us in its grip and will not let go until our very lifeblood is drained and we lie emotionally exhausted. Guilt can tie us to a whipping post and beat us until we feel like we can't go on or don't want to.

How can we break free of its grip? How can we be set free to experience all God has for us? Robert McGee writes in *The Search for Significance:*

"John 10:10 reminds us of how much God treasures His creation, in that Christ came so that man might experience abundant life. However, as Christians, we need to realize that this abundant life is lived in a real world filled with pain, rejection, and failure. Therefore, experiencing the abundant life God intends for us does not mean that our lives will be problem-free. On the contrary, life itself is a series of problems that often act as obstacles in our search for significance, and the abundant life is the experience of God's love, forgiveness, and power in the midst of these problems."[1]

God is truth! Satan is a liar!

For those of us who struggle with our personhood—the very people God created us to be—it is likely we are buying into the lies of the enemy of our souls and coming up short. Our emotional

---

[1] Robert S. McGee, *The Search for Significance* (Nashville, TN: W Publishing Group, a Division of Thomas Nelson Inc. 2003)

bank accounts are bankrupt. How long will we allow ourselves to be deceived by the messenger of Satan and allow him to torment us (2 Corinthians 12:7)?

God did not create us to be placed on the rubbish heap of bruised and battered self-images. He created us in His image. We are loved and esteemed in His sight. He has a wonderful plan for each of our lives; plans to give us hope and a future (Jeremiah 29:11).

Thus, God is our only hope of redemption from guilt and its snares that bind us. And it is His desire that we be set free from this albatross that weighs on us until we are stooped with remorse and self-loathing. Even though our lives will never be problem-free, we need to cut the tie that binds us so we can move forward, unencumbered by feelings of blame and shame. We need to let God make us...

Broken unto Wholeness.

MY JOURNEY

"The truth will set you free" (John 8:32).

My difficult journey really began before we left North Carolina on September 6, 2012. Thus, I was greeted in Kentucky already struggling to maintain and establish myself in our new surroundings. However, it brought forth deep pain and anguish I didn't understand or comprehend. God used my dear loving husband Gary, in untold ways that brought healing to not only my physical well-being, but also to my spiritual well-being.

The next days, weeks, and months began a journey that brought a myriad of doctor visits, specialist visits, blood tests, X-rays, MRIs, CAT scans, etc. Those visits and tests still have not come to a conclusion. As my Primary Care doctor told Gary and me, the countless testing became a process of eliminating maladies rather than discovering them. I spent three days in St. Joseph Hospital in Lexington as they attempted to replenish my malnourished body on its pathway toward healing.

The first night in the hospital, January 22, 2013, God truly used His instrument of healing to bring understanding and insight to my worn and weary body. Dr. Estridge spent an hour and a half ministering insight and awareness at a level I was totally unaware of. We talked about the difference between being sad, depressed, and grieving.

After having experienced two serious depressions in my life, I had sworn I was not depressed. Gary agreed. However, as Dr. Estridge shared—much to my dismay—I became aware that I was indeed in a depression that had slithered under the back door of my soul, squandering my health and peace of mind. The next morning

Dr. Estridge was again at my bedside to make certain I was on the pathway toward healing.

Unfortunately, my IV machine had buzzed every fifteen to twenty minutes during the night, making rest irretrievable. However, I did not feel anguish or anger, but spent the entire night praying to Jesus (His crucifix) on the wall directly facing my bed. That time became extremely significant in my life as the wounded Jesus brought me into a deeper relationship with the risen Christ.

It was as a result of that time spent in solitude with my Lord that I came to understand and accept that I truly was in some state of depression, and I consciously surrendered myself to God's healing power. I believe the time spent with Dr. Estridge transformed my life and my gratitude shall always remain unfailing.

Upon my return home—as I processed this episode in my life—I called Dr. Estridge, and he consented to come to our home to help me gain more awareness on my pathway toward healing. In this day of technology, we are still amazed that a doctor would be willing to make a house call at no charge. He truly was a gift from a heavenly Father who cares.

As we attempted to discern the root of what had plagued my soul—without my knowledge or permission—I became acutely and painfully aware that: "Death had stalked me most of my life." First, with my sister and father; and then with two dear friends, Janice and Carol; and my beloved kitty, Pooh Bear. While Donna lie unconscious, I prayed incessantly that the Person in the heights of heaven would save her so we could be reconciled following a childhood quarrel. However, much to my dismay, she died, abandoning me with over six decades of guilt and remorse.

My mother was driving the car which precipitated her own woundedness for the remainder of her days on earth. In fact, she confessed to her pastor in her last fleeting moments that she was afraid to die lest Donna still be angry with her. Torment had stalked her most of her adult life, until she drew her last breath.

After accepting Jesus as my personal Lord and Savior on November 8th, 1972, I began the journey toward healing and wholeness. However, over four decades later, I am embarrassed to confess that I still struggle with guilt that robbed me of the joy of living much of my adult life. But much to my delight, God has not only used that most sorrowful experience to put me on a path toward healing, but also I have been able to minister to other wounded souls and witness them come into their personal healing. I have found no greater fulfillment in life than to be used by my Lord to bring other wounded souls into a personal relationship with Him and into His healing presence.

Upon contemplation, I came to the realization that I had been robbed of closure with my father—whom Gary and I had the honor and privilege of leading to the Savior of his soul. As well, I had not been able to bring my relationship with my sister Donna, to closure. And after having struggled with the lack of nurturing I was deprived of as a child, I learned that through the awareness of my parents' lack of nurturing, healing had brought me to a place of reconciliation where it was my desire to have my relationship with them restored.

Thus, I planned a celebration party as a symbol of my forgiveness for not meeting my needs, which I had finally comprehended they were unable to meet. But the night before they were to arrive at our home in Illinois, my father dropped dead of a heart attack.

A few years later, without my knowledge of her illness, my dear friend Janice succumbed with my inability to bring our relationship to closure. The shock of her death continues to haunt me to this day. And in 2005, I am still ashamed to admit that—due to a lack of hope or the prospect of a pleasant future—in order to be set free from the pain I was feeling, I attempted to take my life, once again being *stalked by death*. I have come to understand that I really did not want to die. I simply wanted the pain to stop.

And then my dear, dear friend Carol went to meet her Lord unexpectedly without my being able to bring our relationship to closure. As I contemplated the history of *death stalking my life,* rather than having feelings of anger or anxiousness, I feel deep remorse that my loved ones left this earth without my having the privilege of affirming their role in my life and how God had used them to help mold me into the person He created me to be. As a result of Carol's untimely passing, I discerned that, indeed, I was not in a depression but rather grieving for loved ones lost. A quote by Maria Saunders says, "In order to obtain our destiny, it is imperative to birth a closure to the past."

My sorrow remains to this day. How could a loving heavenly Father allow these trials to permeate my spirit? I am anticipating sharing my heart with each of them when we all dwell together in the mansion being prepared for us on streets of gold leading to eternal wholeness with the Savior of our souls, the Lord Jesus Christ.

The toll it took on my life cost me, but not as much as the price my Savior paid to set me free. And a dividend I reaped in the process is the gift of a caring heart for wounded souls. So many people have experienced tragedy in their lives, and some get stuck in their pain and woundedness and are unable to receive God's restorative work.

My scriptural motto has become, "God can use *all* things to bring honor and glory to Him for those who love Him" (Romans 8:28). "Father, I do love You with all my heart and with all my soul and with all my mind and with all my strength" (Mark 12:30). "And I seek to be a vessel of honor for Your glory. My prayer is that I can be an instrument of healing to bring fellow sojourners who share sorrow beyond comprehension."

Several years ago, I believe God spoke to my spirit about writing a book entitled *Broken unto Wholeness*. My subtitle is *Wounded Soldiers Marching toward Victory*. "Oh, dear God, please help me be obedient to Your Call on my life that I might bring honor and glory to You who blesses all Your children with Your presence and loving-kindness."

We are all wounded souls in one way or another. Jesus sacrificed His life that we might be set free from those things that bind us and inhibit our ability to be set free, indeed. Won't you join me on this quest as our brokenness is made whole for the sake of the One who gave His life for you and for me?

I am grateful for these events that brought me to a place of not only *hope* but also *insight* for a future bright with joy unspeakable and full of glory. An additional gift from the Lord was when—as I was discharged from St. Joseph Hospital in Lexington—the door was opened for me to become part of the Associate Chaplain Ministry in which I had also served at Mission Hospital in Asheville. God is good beyond measure and faithful to His Word. However, prolonged illness has prevented me from fulfilling this opportunity.

After further contemplation, I am realizing that—as Gary and I had supposed—I was not in a depression, but rather still grieving for my dear friend Carol, whose loss affected my life deeply. The incapability to bring closure to our relationship left a wound that has not yet healed. Her dear husband Mark, has assured me of her deep love for me, and I assured him that my love for her shall never wane. Visiting her burial ground and touching her memorial stone were touch points toward my healing.

Thus, I continue my quest of being made *broken unto wholeness*. I trust the Savior of my soul will assist this wounded soldier on her march toward victory.

A LONG ROAD

Marilyn was hospitalized from February 12 to May 6, 2017.

Gary:

> "This was the most profound, painful time in my
> life." February 2013
> No Closures

> "This was the most profound, painful time in my
> life." February 2016
> Urinary Tract Infections

> "This was the most profound, painful time in my
> life." February 2017
> Seizures

My husband Gary wrote the following:

It all started with *The Dance.* It was February 12, 1960. Marilyn was the new girl in school (and the prettiest cheerleader), and I was the shy guy that asked her to the Valentine's Dance. She sometimes reminds me that I didn't even hold her hand. Only God could know where that first date would take us in the years ahead.

Fast forward to Sunday night, February 12, 2017. Now married to my high school sweetheart for over fifty-five years, we were looking forward to what lies ahead for our future. Unfortunately, Marilyn spent almost the next three months in St. Joseph Hospital in Lexington, Kentucky; Cardinal Hill, a short-term rehabilitation hospital; and Lexington Country Place, a long-term rehabilitation center; trying to regain her physical strength and learning to walk again after four seizures while in the hospital.

Needless to say, that was not what we were expecting our future to hold. Except for God Almighty and the Savior of our souls, Jesus, we did not know if we could survive this dark night of our souls. But praise be to God, we have survived and look forward to serving Him for the rest of our days on this earth—before spending eternity with the One Who holds our futures. By His Holy Spirit, our lives will be fruitful and honorable to the One to Whom we have entrusted our futures.

2017: Praise the Lord, it's over!
2017: We rebuke February!
2018: Better days lie ahead!

To God be the glory for what He is doing!

MY PLACE

"So if the Son sets you free, you will be free indeed"
(John 8:36).

The origin of my first *place* was Clarion, Iowa, where I was born on August 27, 1943. I have come to realize that I possibly did not have a sense of belonging from the time I was placed in my mother's arms, and I have wandered throughout my life looking for a *place* to be.

There have been, of course, places in my life, some of which, for one reason or another, have passed without my consent. Growing up on a farm in Iowa produced—along with crops and animals—its own sense of isolation.

In those early days, I now realize my sister Donna—seventeen months older than me—was a significant *place* in my life. But when I was ten, she tragically died in a car accident and so, too, died my *place* with her. I spent the remainder of my childhood on the farm feeling alone and isolated, seeking a *place* to be.

I subsequently learned that I had not lived up to my parents' expectations of being born a male child. A few years ago, I learned that my mother had not wanted another child so soon after my sister. My sense of identity was shattered, lying in ruins at the bottom of my soul. I felt like I was going round and around—like a goldfish—finding nothing but itself. Resurrection would come through pain and toil. His Name is Jesus.

A few years ago, my brother took me on a tour of our old homestead. Much to my dismay, the farmhouse and all the other buildings had been demolished and laid to rest. An important part of me had died, and I wasn't even aware of its death. Grieving had not been given permission to mourn. Bro Ron is a special link to my family heritage.

Gary and I met in our junior year of high school. I was immediately drawn to him, but did not realize until recently the significance of him becoming a *place* in my desolate wasteland, searching to find my *place* on this earth.

In some respects—looking back on it now—moving to Illinois from Iowa after his graduation from college was like moving away from roots that had not taken root. A sense of rootlessness has plagued my entire adult life, never to be replanted with fruition.

Being married and having children did not fill that void until I accepted Jesus as my Savior on November 8, 1972. He transformed my life, and I was filled with indescribable joy and a peace that surpasses understanding. He gave my life meaning and purpose for living. However, the emptiness I had felt within the depths of my soul soon turned those early days of my salvation into torment I still struggle with today. Depression became hopelessness in my life as a result of deprivation of love as a child.

My toddler days as a Christian were the most enriching and fulfilling days of my adult life—finding my *place*, growing in the unconditional love of my Lord Jesus Christ, and sharing Him with those who crossed my path. The joy of leading others to Jesus and observing the transformation in their lives gave me a sense of belonging, and hence a *place* to be.

I do believe God spoke audibly to me about our moving to North Carolina. However, I did not realize it would become a wilderness experience that made me feel like I had been robbed of my joy and purpose for living. It took me several years to realize that I was living in a foreign land—feeling like an exile with no *place* to be—which brought back subconscious memories of feeling like an exile, even in my family of origin.

My deep sense of rootlessness eventually brought me to such depth of depletion as a human soul that I lost my desire to live. I felt like hope had eluded me—never to be recaptured—and the very thought of it drove me to unconsciousness. My hopelessness lay in a pool of vomit on the bathroom floor. It was only then that the pieces of my life began to weave back together. God had allowed me to be broken to make me whole, and He has used and is continuing to use my woundedness as a healing agent in the lives of others. However, with great pain, I have still not found my *place*. And even more so, I felt and feel alone and isolated in a *place* called home.

It seems difficult to understand that kind of profound pain when my dear husband has stood by my side and been a haven of strength and encouragement for over five decades. The lack of nurturing in my early years has continued to wreak havoc in my psyche. But I have learned that no one person—even the one who loves me most in this world—can fill the void that has stalked my life. And the loss of other significant people have only accentuated the void I feel deep within my soul—which brings me in touch with the void of yesteryear—negating a sense of self-worth and value in an uncaring world.

My profound grief at a dear friend's wake helped me realize that dying, too, has a *place* in living. It is also a *place*—touchstone, if you will—in our relationship with others. My friend was a *place* in my life and, along with her death, a part of me died, also. I have not only experienced deep grief for her loss but for mine, as well. Carol was a link to my spiritual heritage.

And my dear, dear friend Sarah. What a saint of God! She was ninety-six years old when she went home to the *place* God had prepared for her. She was a pastor's wife for thirty years before becoming a widow. And she was a *place* in my life in North Carolina. Our bond was woven with love, caring, support, and respect for each other. I say was because, after being given anesthesia for hip surgery in May of 2010, she developed dementia and it felt like I had lost her. It was one of the most painful experiences of my life.

Gary and I visited her at the nursing home every other Sunday. She still knew us, but her soul was all that truly lived. It broke my heart. Though most of what she said was not discernable, she could still recite Scripture with me as I read from my mother's Bible Promise Book, lift praises to the Lord from her innermost being, and sing hymns of old with Gary. She is a treasure that shall never tarnish and shall always live in our hearts.

Paul Tournier's book, *A Place for You,* has been a catalyst in this writing. You have probably noticed that it seems like I have not had a *place* in my surroundings. He writes, "The ideal *place* for the child is the family. When the family is such that the child cannot fit himself into it properly, he looks everywhere for some other *place*, leading a wandering existence incapable of settling down anywhere.

"The child who has been able to grow up harmoniously in a healthy home finds a welcome everywhere. Later on, wherever he goes, he will be able to make any *place* his own, without any effort on his part. He, who has once had the experience of belonging in a *place*, always finds a *place* for himself afterward; whereas he who has been deprived of it, searches everywhere in vain."

I am still searching.

He goes on to share, "A surgeon referred to the problem of those who have had a limb amputated. Even when we have a tooth out, we do not feel the same as before, and we cannot keep our tongue away from the fascinating void. The man who has lost a limb has lost his *place*. He must adapt himself to a new *place*."[2] I find it intriguing that Dr. Tournier refers to having a tooth out can give us a sense of losing our *place*. I am having a tooth uprooted in February. Unwittingly, I will again have lost a *place* in my life.

As already stated, in my formative years I experienced deprivation of love, and thus a deprivation of *place*. Through it all, I have come to learn that uprootedness—being uprooted from the very things that give us a *place* to be—wounds us in ways that only the Lord and Maker of mankind can bring resolution and healing. My most earnest desire is to be a wounded healer so that other sojourners might walk in liberty and become agents of healing to hurting souls who cross their path.

To God be the glory for all He is doing in my life, as I strive to find my *place* in His creation! I look forward with great anticipation and expectation to spending eternity with my Lord and Savior Jesus Christ in heaven, my eternal *place*.

January 16, 2012

---

[2] Paul Tournier, *A Place for You* (Harper Collins, 1968)

MANURE TO COUNTY SUPERVISOR

Received Phone Calls from Two Presidents
Went Bankrupt!

My father, Gene Sturgeon, was someone I looked up to and admired. He had to quit school his sophomore year to help take care of his six sisters after their father died of a heart attack.

My mother, Mabel Sturgeon, grew up in very difficult circumstances. She grew up on a farm in central Iowa with two brothers. My grandmother had severe diabetes and needed to be cared for herself. Thus, my mother had to assume responsibility far too young—before becoming an adult. She was not allowed to marry until she was twenty-one.

My parents were wed on New Year's Day in 1941. My father was a farmer and worked long hours to make a livelihood for our family. Thus, he was not available to us as much as we needed.

He was well-respected in our community and was one of the first to build a cattle confinement setup. However, when the bottom dropped out of the cattle market—much to his chagrin—he was forced to file for bankruptcy.

He ran for county Supervisor and was elected. He was very successful in meeting the needs of his constituents and was elected for a second term. During that time, he received phone calls from both Republican President Ronald Reagan and Democratic President Jimmy Carter. In fact, during one of the elections, Gary and I were able to attend and watch the votes come in. Dad won! God made him *broken unto wholeness*. One of the most meaningful things in my life was the privilege of leading him to the Lord Jesus.

As his daughter, I am extremely proud of him. He died much too soon. In fact, as I wrote earlier, he passed away the night before my parents were to come to our home in Illinois for a celebration of who they were in my life. I shall always be indebted for the role model my father was. Bless him, dear Lord, as he rests in You.

SINFUL NATURES

For all have sinned and fall short of the glory of God. (Romans 3:23)

Mankind is broken. Human beings are born into this world depraved—with sinful natures. No matter how much we want or how hard we try, we fall short of the glory of God. However, He sacrificially sent His one and only Son into the world to redeem us from eternal punishment. Jesus was born to die that you and I might live. He came to make us *broken unto wholeness.*

It is God's will that none perish but have everlasting life. It is also not His will that we live our lives brokenhearted—succumbing to the trials of life—no matter how difficult or painful they are. Our vision is so limited, but we must remember to keep our eyes focused on God's vision for our lives. Romans 8:28 tells us, "And we know that in *all* things God works for the good of those who love Him, who have been called according to His purpose."

Sometimes what seems bad to us—or failure we cannot resurrect—God is able to turn into good beyond what we could ever imagine or dream. Dreams are our hope for the future, and God's Word says He came to give us hope and a future (Jeremiah 29:11). Don't let the nightmares of your life become the measuring stick of what your future holds. Rather, look to the One who holds your future.

God is full of mercy and grace. His loving-kindness far outreaches our greatest expectations. He is a God of compassion Who never fails. His desire is for you to become all He created you to be, not stuck in the muck and mire of evil deeds that paralyze you from moving into a productive, happy life.

Please take hold of His Hand. He is reaching out to you. He is waiting for you to relinquish control of your life and your circumstances, and allow Him to make you *broken unto wholeness*. All of Humpty Dumpty's men could not put him together again. But God created you and He knows how all the pieces of your life fit together. He does all things well, and He will not fail you! He never fails! He is trustworthy! We must hold firmly to the trustworthy message we have been taught. It will sustain us when everything else saps us of our energy and well-being.

INSPIRATION

> We remember before our God and Father your
> work produced by faith, your labor prompted by
> love, and your endurance inspired by hope in our
> Lord Jesus Christ. (1 Thessalonians 1:3)

Who inspires you? Who do you inspire? Inspiration is a catalyst that can move us from a place of feeling stuck, to moving us into the creativity that is bred in the very depths of our being that God created us to be. There is something within that cries out to be released, and our souls shall not rest until our dreams are fulfilled.

Of course, there are many people in the Bible who inspire us and also inspired those in their time—foremost, our Lord and Savior Jesus Christ. He is the only true Source of our inspiration. His example of molding the disciples still influences our lives today. A few other examples were Moses' tremendous impact on the lives of David, and then Jonathan. Also Timothy on the life of Titus, and James' address to Christians everywhere. These models of inspiration in the Word of God stand as testaments for us today.

Our works are produced by faith. Jesus is the author and finisher of all that we achieve in this life. Our love for Jesus to be obedient to His calling prompts us to strive to accomplish His purpose for our lives. Our perseverance permeates hope within our souls to accomplish that which He has called us to do so that He will be glorified. Our inspiration also gives us an opportunity to inspire others. Who do you inspire today?

> Without His love, I can do nothing.
> With His love, there is nothing I cannot do.

—Unknown

DANCING AT MY FUNERAL

by
Maxie Dunnam
(Copyright Permission Granted)

A Note of Explanation:

Only one year after I invited Jesus into my heart, I suffered a severe depression, putting me in a psychiatric ward for five days just before Christmas—with two small children—not wanting to live. It was the most profound, damning experience of my life.

However, one of the tools God used to put me on the path to being made *broken unto wholeness* was Maxie Dunnam's book, *Dancing At My Funeral.* Thus my reason for including this chapter. I would encourage you to read it in contrast to my experience. I pray that it might also lead you to deal with your *hounds of hell* that our caring heavenly Father desires to heal through the *Hound of Heaven.* May His Holy Spirit draw you to accept Jesus as the Lord and Savior of your life. It is my prayer that, from now to eternity, you will experience healing of your memories, as Maxie and I have. To God be all glory and honor, both now and forevermore.

Marilyn

"*Dancing At My Funeral* is a book of autobiography, personal history, and deep feelings. It takes into account the fact that all of us are a very real product of those early shaping forces in our lives. Maxie is now free by the grace of God to look back and to look within and to literally dance at the funeral of the past that has haunted him. He now finds in his past the fruitful seeds of his new life and his new ministry. The past for all of us is not something to be hidden, but something to be celebrated. He reminds us that our Lord said that the Kingdom of God is within. It is within us that we begin to find the truest understanding of the shape of grace and of the new creation." Won't you look within and dance? (from the foreword by Bruce Larson)

Maxie says, "Funerals are about death; dancing is about life. My trip is *dancing at my funeral.* Dancing when I have the courage to resist forces that would bury me... Dancing when I bury some part of me that doesn't deserve to live...dancing in the face of tragedy over which I have no control except to trust God and life and circumstance."

He calls dancing at his funeral a process in which he learns to experience life with a freshness and a sense of purpose. And though he purposefully avoids pat answers, he shares his formula for making authentic Christian living a viable, realistic possibility.

A DANCING TRIP

Yes, I'm on a *dancing* trip! That's odd, really, for I have no technical knowledge of dancing nor is *the dance* part of my culture. For me, dancing is a symbol, and I hope that as you read, you'll come to understand this symbol and why it is so important to me. I *feel* it! Deep down, I feel it!

But about the title. Am I dancing at my *funeral?* Yes!

Funerals I know about. I've always known about them. In rural Mississippi, we weren't protected from whatever damage they're supposed to inflict upon children. Funerals were part of our culture, like going to town on Saturday, Fourth-Sunday sings, summer revival meetings, cakewalks at school socials, and smoking rabbit tobacco behind the barn. Also, as a minister, I've conducted hundreds of funerals.

Funerals are about death. Death has many faces. One face is *spiritual* death, the things within us that must die if we are to live. Features of this face include resentment, guilt, self-hate, and remorse. These things will cripple us, make us less than men and women— and prematurely bury us if we do not bury them. And then there is *physical* death, over which we may have little control and ultimately have *no* control. An accident stamps out a life, or a life passes in a natural way. Someone we love is with us no more. And our own death—we can't understand that until it happens.

Funerals are about death; *dancing* is about life. My trip is *dancing at my funeral.* Dancing when I have the courage to resist forces that would bury me and am somehow given the power to bury them, instead. Dancing when I bury some part of me that doesn't deserve to live—some ritual that is no longer meaningful, some security blanket that no longer supports, some phony approach to life, some superficial relationship, some crutch, or game, or mask.

I am dancing in the face of tragedy over which I have no control except to trust God and life and circumstance. I am able to live in the presence of death because I trust myself as a victor rather than a victim.

The dance and the funeral are *symbols* for my trip. But symbols may be very real!

"I invite you to join me on my trip. Dance with me!" I want to, Maxie.

Maxie Dunnam
Anaheim, California
1973

OLD PAPPY TIME IS A PICKING MY POCKET

The ridiculous and the sublime of our experience often are bound together by a cord of memory—you recall the one and the other comes sliding out of its storage rack and replays, too.

Whenever I read the 90th Psalm, which I often do at funerals, the congregation must think it strange when a half-smile plays across my face. This expression is inappropriate and unintended. What happens is that this sublime Psalm invariably triggers a replaying of a ridiculous song which I heard on a cold winter's night many years ago.

It may have been during the Christmas holidays—at any rate, I was driving from Mississippi to Georgia. I became exhausted, and fearing that I might doze off, I stopped at a roadside cafe to energize myself with coffee.

I'm not talking about a Howard Johnson-type of restaurant, but a truck stop. You know the type, standing there alongside a desolate stretch of road, slumbering by day but coming alive at night to beckon you with its winking neon eyes.

Maybe it's just me, but loneliness seems to pervade such places and the people who frequent them. There's always a jukebox, and it's packed with loneliness, too. Its songs tell of hurt and heartbreak, unrequited love and lost hopes. I'm not knocking these songs, understand. Some deal with life rather authentically. For example, when Bobbie Gentry sings "Ode to Billie Joe," you share the hurt, frustration, and guilt of the bereft young lover even though you've likely never been near the fateful Tallahatchie River Bridge. Each of us has his or her own Tallahatchie Bridge.

Although it's been fully fifteen years since I stopped in at that roadside cafe, the song that I heard there keeps coming back to mind. I had never heard it before and I've never heard it since. I don't remember the words, but I remember the tune, the twanging, nasal voice of the singer, and the oft-repeated title line: "Old Pappy Time Is A Picking My Pocket."

This song wasn't a classical art form; nevertheless, there's an immortal thought in that title, "Old Pappy Time Is A Picking My Pocket," and it has been a burr under the saddle of my memory all these years.

But back to the sublime, the 90th Psalm. Do you remember how it goes?

90th Psalm:

> Lord, thou hast been our dwelling place
> in all generations.
> Before the mountains were brought forth, or
> ever thou hadst formed the earth and the
> world, from everlasting to everlasting
> thou art God.
>
> For a thousand years in thy sight
> are but as yesterday when it is past,
>
> like grass which is renewed in the morning:
> in the morning it flourishes and is renewed;
> in the evening it fades and withers.
>
> Our years come to an end like a sigh.
>
> So teach us to number our days
> that we may get a heart of wisdom.
>
> (Verses 1, 2, 4, 5, 6, 9, 12 RSV)

"Old Pappy Time Is A Picking My Pocket" is a ridiculous song. Who remembers it? The 90th Psalm is sublime literature which has endured through the ages. It's strange that I would associate these two, isn't it? Yet, I believe it's like this in our experience. If we will tear off the pretentious, protective wrapping and get to the core of our life-package, we will find there a strange mixture of beauty and ugliness, ecstasy and agony.

But we are not helplessly stuffed with these things. Indeed, I am walking evidence that the hell that is inside us can be turned into heaven. This is why I am writing this book.

My change came about in the most unsuspected and even implausible way. I was going to my funeral but instead experienced my resurrection. You see, Old Pappy Time had picked my pocket for a long, long time. I don't mean that he was shoving me into fearsome old age—what he was doing was sucking out my life-juices. The unresolved conflicts of my past sapped my vitality so that I was unable to live vibrantly in the present or to contemplate the future without anxiety.

I knew with my *mind* that we can only live in the present, but that was not my *experience*. Indeed, I was stuck in my past as though my feet were planted in concrete.

There are immature and destructive ways in which people can deal with their past. One is to glory in the past as if it were some golden age which, alas, will never return. With such an attitude, we linger in the fantasies of yesterday and refuse to move up into the realities of today. And if living in the present is difficult, relating to the future is an impossibility.

My problem was just the opposite. I didn't love the past, I *hated* it. I'm not talking about hating isolated parts of my past. I hated the whole bundle. I wanted to bury my past, but I didn't respect it sufficiently to give it a decent funeral.

Some people describe themselves as *children of the Depression*, meaning they were shaped by the economic era which began with the suicide-generating crash of 1929 and continued well into the New Deal. In 1934, when I was born, economic ruin still marred the face of Perry County, Mississippi.

But I suffered my depression later and in another place. My depression came over me when I moved beyond the confines of Perry County. Travel, college, and seminary provided me with windows through which I looked out upon a bright, rich world. But when I looked out the rearward windows and into my past, I saw a dull, deprived world. I felt that as a kid I had been cheated. I became resentful and bitter. Thoughts of my past put a rancid taste in my mouth.

I remember the one suit, one white shirt, and one tie with which I went to college. The suit was the least expensive that we could find in Richton. (These were not depression days, but 1951.) The occasion for its purchase was the high school senior class play. I was cast as the father of two teenagers, and I had to wear a suit appropriate for my stage age.

Maybe you can imagine how I felt the first week of college when I arrived at a fraternity rush party in my drab, middle-aged attire. Amid snappily dressed college dons, I stood out like a sore thumb. That experience was one among many that caused my resentment and bitterness to grow.

I had already begun my proving game. Despite feelings of miserable out-of-placeness, I stuck with the fraternity bit until after I had been initiated. Then I dropped. The feelings of not belonging were too great. I had proved something, however. I had proved that I *could* be a fraternity man. That pattern of empty proving was to continue for many years.

Francis Thompson experienced a *Hound of Heaven*, the incessant love of God following him. I'm sure that was my experience, too. But another *hound* was far more real to me most of the time—a *hound of hell*. This hound, my past, dogged my heels. Its barking threatened to reveal who I really was—a limited, underdeveloped, uncultured, unsophisticated exile from rural Mississippi. Internally, I began minimizing the progress that I had made. I came to feel that the only difference between then and now was that now I was wearing shoes.

Cold words on a cold page cannot recreate the desperation which I suffered. Thoughts of my personal history put a rancid taste in my mouth. And although your past is no doubt different from mine, perhaps there is in your history some unresolved conflict that sends shudders up and down your spine. If so, it will help you to understand what I'm saying.

Here is how Henri Percikow in "Childhood" expressed the feelings I'm trying to share:

> Can I forget—
> The barren chalked garret
> In which we huddled,
> Curling from cold,
> Fighting for the shifting coats?
> Can I forget—
> The stinking cellar
> where sunshine was alien
> And the orange crate bare?
>
> Can I forget—
> Mother, nursing the lame
> washing the ghetto dead—
> For scanty crumbs?
> I can't forget
> When still trapped
> On the hook of greed
> Warding off the hurt
> Of the desperate claws.

Mine was a different sort of ghetto, although it had claws which raked across my soul.

In my preadolescent days, we lived in a three-room *shotgun* house. There was a kitchen, a living room with a bed in it, and another room with two beds. I was the youngest of five children, and often I slept with the two just older than me. The heater in the living room ravenously devoured the wood that I brought in but gave out pitifully little warmth in exchange. My ghetto had grassless yards, dilapidated cars, sagging porches, and barns whose pungent odors penetrated the kitchen when the wind was blowing wrong. The toilet was inconveniently reached by a path. The *joys* of my ghetto included *commodity* butter and hand-me-down overalls. Dried lima beans were our staple food four or five times a week. A food celebration was Sunday dinner with a chicken killed from our yard. We were late getting government electricity; I read by kerosene lamp until I was in the fifth grade.

Although my life-poverty originated chiefly out of economics and geography, poverty doesn't depend upon either of these elements. For example, perhaps you yourself have endured interminable stretches of empty time, and the memory of this nothingness haunts you nowadays as a wasteland can continue to mock a parched traveler long after his rescue. Most cases of life-poverty seem to have sprung out of broken relationships. Perhaps your relationship with one or more of your parents or siblings have left you upset or unfulfilled. Are you carrying around inside you the jagged pieces of a shattered love affair or a smashed career? Do you suffer guilt because you hurt someone? Has the door to reconciliation or recovery seemingly been slammed shut by someone's death or financial collapse?

Although the terrible event itself is back there in the past, the disappointment, hurt, bitterness, or remorse which you feel is in the present. It is excruciatingly real, isn't it?

To banish the past, we can employ *repression*. I doubt that anyone has tried to repress the past (push it back even beyond consciousness) any more than I have. But repression doesn't work. There's a sinister power within the past which enables it to come twisting and contorting out of the depths of our being and into our thoughts no matter how hard we try to forget.

We can also try to overcome the past by running (and how I have run!). Some people run in disreputable ways—they take drugs, engage in illicit sex, or abandon their family. Some run in socially acceptable ways—they scramble up the ladder of success and establish a home in the suburbs, gathering for themselves and their children a portfolio of credentials via education and memberships. They run after *the good things in life* which they couldn't afford in the past and which many *other* people can't afford in the present.

My past was pursuing me like a hound of hell, and I ran!

In countless past encounters, this hound had slashed and torn me. He was always out there somewhere, sniffing me out. I lived in dread of his next attack.

Finally, it became apparent to me that I would either move to slay this beast or he would devour me. But from the temporary successes that I had experienced over the years, I recognized that I couldn't expect to rescue myself in one fell swoop; instead, I would have to begin a long and painful process. I had to convince myself that of itself the past wasn't terrifying—I was letting the past unnerve me as a child is terrorized by shadows on a bedroom wall.

The first serious step in my process of inner self-communication I took quite deliberately. I blocked out two days on my calendar and obtained use of a cabin way back in the mountains.

Being a *modern* man, I had always assumed that without noise and activity, nothing was happening. This was one of the reasons why I'd never been alone with myself for long—it seemed unproductive. Another reason was that I was afraid to be alone with myself. And although I recommend the process highly, let me caution you that until you have tried being alone and apart for two days, you have no conception of the stillness, emptiness, and penetrating loneliness.

Although my purpose was clear, I attempted to shield myself that first morning by engaging in *busy* activities. I cleaned the cabin and filled potholes in the road. Slowly, I became able to throw off my everyday compulsions and inhibitions. I ran through tall grass, waded in a cold stream, skipped rocks across a crystal pool nestled under a powerful waterfall. I wafted leaves off a cliff and watched them float to a new resting place.

I was a tow-headed boy again—barefoot, shirtless. Memories of hours spent alone on a creek bank waiting for a fish to take my bait flooded in. Being alone *then* hadn't been painful, I reflected. Why *now*?

I was becoming more at peace with myself, and finally I found courage to throw myself into my task.

It was then that those two days really became *mine*. I remembered, reflected, prayed. I cried, screamed, kicked rocks, pounded on my pillow. At other times, I recited poetry aloud or sang. All the while I was recollecting, sorting out, throwing away, keeping.

It happened the second night. It was cold and I hugged the fireplace. It was also near Christmas. Perhaps it was these connections that conjured up this relic of my past, the roadside cafe. It appeared as I saw myself driving down a desolate road. I went inside. The customers and waitresses stood or sat lifeless, like wax figures in a museum. I looked into their empty faces. Meanwhile, I was pained by the unbearable silence of the place.

There was the click of a coin and the whirring of machinery, and out of the jukebox came that loud, twanging voice singing "Old Pappy Time Is A Picking My Pocket."

In a twinkling, the scene was gone—the curtain of my memory-theater came down. Once again I was in the cabin, alone and chilled. But there had been in that tableau a message for me, and the message remained with me.

For the first time, I saw that my past had power to undo me because I myself was energizing it. My past was *back there*, frozen in time as were these figures in the roadside cafe. The past couldn't hurt me unless I *let* it hurt me.

That night I was able to call to my mind's stage many events of the past which I had never before permitted myself to view objectively. Some memories caused me to wince, but seeing them in perspective permitted me to deal with them without either wallowing in remorse or withdrawing in pain.

I had achieved what I had come to the mountains to accomplish: to deal with my history and to purge my mind and cleanse my soul. I had stopped in my tracks and I had turned and faced that hound of hell. To my delight, I discovered that he had stopped, too. He didn't go away, but he didn't unnerve me any longer.

I became able to accept and appreciate my past. There were parts of it, I discovered, which I wanted to keep alive; there were other parts which I wanted to bury. And in this "funeral" process, I began to experience life with a freshness and a sense of purpose that had eluded me.

I was dancing at my funeral.

I came down from the mountain to my family, to begin a new life with them.

One evening not long after my mountaintop experience, I went shopping alone. In the midst of the hustle and bustle of a toy department, I felt the cold nose and hot breath of that hound of hell once again. I recalled scraggly Christmas trees, near-empty stockings, and turkey-less tables. However, I was able to call up the resources that I had gained in the mountains. Through the same process of examination, acceptance, sifting out, and putting into perspective, I was able to cope with the feelings of loneliness and resentment of this later encounter. Not only was I able to free myself, but even to rise to a higher level of self-appreciation and confidence.

On my way home, I reflected upon what had happened. Upon arriving home, I set down these lines:

> I was a child again
>> but not really a child
>
> I was a man-child
>> reduced to fantasy
>> and speechless awe
>> by what I saw
>
> The Indy 500
>> was a far cry
>> from the homemade truck
>> a board for a body
>> a tin can for a cab
>
> Magnet chess and checker pieces
>> that hold to shiny boards
>> were far out front
>> of games played with buttons
>> on squares penciled
>> on a cardboard box

Even the tic-tac-toe
    was in fine garb
    x's and o's in tuxedos
    standing at attention
    in squares neatly
    scored on wooden plaques
    instead of x's and o's
    in common dress
    standing at ease
    in irregular spaces
    laid out by a stubby pencil

There was Monopoly and Aggravation
    and Red Baron and hundreds of
    other games of chance and skill

There were Hot Wheels and Korny Kars
    and Tonkas and Matchboxes
It was another world
    and I was a child again

None of these fantastic toys
    had ever been mine
But I remembered a little track
    about two feet in diameter
    and a little windup train
    creeping around
    (It must have been zooming then)

It provided thrills aplenty
    until the spring
    too tired
    and too tightly wound
    gave up and died

I found it in a dresser drawer
    (We didn't have a tree that year)
    on Christmas morning
    and I knew that Santa came to
    poor boys' homes, too.

I was a child again
    but not really a child
I was a man-child
    reduced to fantasy and awe
    by what I saw

I thanked God for memory
    and parents who tried hard
    and gave all!

That, to me, is life! To be able to look at the past with openness. To be able to deal with gashing wounds as well as gracious gifts. To be able to accept the intimate moments and the utter abandonment. Through my process of self-communication, I had become able to deal with the whole mix of my past.

Now I could acknowledge past events, appreciate them, and appropriate them for present use. I recognized that it was I who had made many decisions which in the past I had chosen to blame on others. My parents hadn't failed me; I made a "bummer" out of my past by resentment. More importantly, I was able to celebrate the fact that here and now I am a *decision-maker!*

The smell of death was giving way to the aroma of life. With Sam Keene in "To A Dancing God," I could say: "Judgement, forgiveness, and gratitude will form the alchemy which transforms the past from fate into fortune and which changes me from being a victim of causes over which I had no control to being a participant in a past which I continually reform."

My conversion and discovery of a new life-style are so precious to me that I want to share them with you. But for the moment, you may find it more profitable to lay this book aside and begin dealing with your own past.

Call up out of your past the things that hound you. Acknowledge them—write them down or discuss them with someone. Be honest. Be specific. Make a thorough self-examination. Once you have done this, pick up this book again and review your situation, using the following questions as guidelines:

- What pain do you feel?
- What joy?
- What confusion?
- What certainty?
- How painful was the memory?
- How crippling?
- How important or superficial?
- What about it do you want to keep?
- What would you like to bury?
- Who are the important persons?
- Whom are you holding responsible?
- Do you need to confess?
- To forgive?
- Is there anything you can do?
- Is there anything you want to do?
- If so, why don't you do it?

Don't repress—acknowledge! Don't run—affirm!

But a word of caution: Don't expect all your problems to vanish in a flash. Remember, self-communication and inner renewal is a *process*, an ongoing enterprise!

When the Psalmist prayed, "So teach us to number our days that we may get a heart of wisdom," he undoubtedly was talking about *all* our days—past, present, future. God is Lord of not only the present and future but also the *past*. Your present will never be the exciting, living-fully-here-and-now experience that you deserve

70

until you confront and grapple with whatever hound of hell has been plaguing you out of the past. And God will help you do it!

If you've been feeling as though you were going to a funeral, remember: You can experience a resurrection!

Living depends on loving,

Loving depends on knowing,

Knowing depends on risking.

May God add His blessing to the words you've just read, and may He put you on a journey of being made *broken unto wholeness*. Amen.

CARING REFLECTIONS

"Pure and genuine in the sight of God the Father means caring for orphans and widows in their distress and refusing to let the world corrupt you" (James 1:27).

QUESTIONS AND ANSWERS

Questions are the gateway
to the answers we seek.

It is to the questions of life that we gain insight and answers for our journey. Answering questions helps us get in touch with who we are and what made us who we are. An unwillingness to answer questions about ourselves could lock doors into our souls—which might never be illumined—while a willingness to answer questions about ourselves could open windows into our souls, shedding light on our hearts and lives. You can't get to the truth by asking the wrong questions.

Ask God to prepare your heart to receive the answers He is waiting to shine on you. If your life is a question mark, let the *Light* of the world become your exclamation point!

This exploration through questions is designed to assist you in searching your heart for the answers that lie within. It can be accomplished by yourself, but could be more effectual by asking someone to join you on the journey, as well as an avenue for small groups to discover and edify each other. Allow God to make you *broken unto wholeness.*

When answers aren't enough, there is Jesus.

—Scott Wesley Brown

I know now, Lord, why You utter no answer.
You are Yourself the Answer.

—C. S. Lewis

HOPE

> "For I know the plans I have for you," declares the Lord, "plans to prosper you and not to harm you, plans to give you hope and a future. Then you will call upon Me and come and pray to Me, and I will listen to you. You will seek Me and find Me when you seek Me with all your heart."
> (Jeremiah 29:11–13)

The word *hope* is rich with blessing. The Word of God is brimming with hope. "Put your hope in the Lord, for with the Lord is unfailing love and with Him is full redemption" (Psalm 130:7).

"Yet this I call to mind and therefore I have hope: because of the Lord's great love we are not consumed, for His compassions never fail. They are new every morning; great is Your faithfulness. I say to myself, 'The Lord is my portion; therefore I will wait for Him.' The Lord is good to those whose hope is in Him, to the one who seeks Him; it is good to wait quietly for the salvation of the Lord" (Lamentations 3:21–26).

"For in this hope we were saved. But hope that is seen is no hope at all. Who hopes for what he already has? But if we hope for what we do not yet have, we wait for it patiently" (Romans 8:24–25).

"May the God of hope fill you with all joy and peace as you trust in Him, so that you may overflow with hope by the power of the Holy Spirit" (Romans 15:13).

"This is the secret: That Christ in your heart is your only hope of glory" (Colossians 1:27 TLB).

Do you have hope? If not, let Jesus transform the hopelessness you feel into His hope for your life. He died that you might live in hope. "Those who hope in the Lord will renew their strength; they will soar on wings like eagles; they will run and not grow weary; they will walk and not be faint" (Isaiah 40:31).

Do you need strength to make it through this day—the battles that wage on every side of your life? Remember, the Lord isn't finished yet. He is waiting to fill you with His hope. His desire is to renew and restore you. Put your hope in God. Your hope comes from Him. Allow Him to make you *broken unto wholeness*.

"We have this hope as an anchor for the soul:
firm and secure" (Hebrews 6:19).

"Blessed is he…whose hope is in the Lord his God" (Psalm 146:5).

"Let us hold unswervingly to the hope we profess, for
He who promised is faithful" (Hebrews 10:23).

Hope is the thing with feathers that perches in the soul,
and sings the tune without words.

—Emily Dickinson

GRACE

Grace, grace, God's grace,
Grace that will pardon and cleanse within.
Grace, grace, God's grace,
Grace that is greater than all our sin.

—Don Moen

Have you experienced the grace of God in your life? His grace is what sustains us during the hard times. As sin runs rampant in this evil world, we often feel sequestered from the peace of God. Sometimes we wonder if we will even survive the test and trials that knock at our door. Jesus tells us clearly in Revelation 3:20, "Here I am! I stand at the door and knock. If anyone hears My voice and opens the door, I will come in and eat with him, and he with Me."

Have you heard Jesus knocking at the door of your heart? Have you opened your door and allowed Him to enter in? Have you shared nourishment with Him, while allowing Him to nurture you with the spirit of His presence? Allow Him to make you *broken unto wholeness.*

So many of us live our lives separated from the One who came to give us abundant life. Without His presence, we feel void of joy and fulfillment in this life. He is offering us sustenance not only for today but also for tomorrow and the rest of our lives. Why would we want to reject the sacrifice He made on our behalf and live less than His best?

Are you shackled by things that have you bound by shreds of cloth that are hindering you from living the abundant life? I'd like to share a portion from Keith Miller and Bruce Larson's book, *The Passionate People.* It is taken from Scripture when Jesus raised Lazarus from the dead.

As Jesus came to the tomb, He called in a loud voice, "Lazarus, come out!" Lazarus came out; his hands and feet wrapped with strips of linen. However, Jesus never got Lazarus out of the grave clothes. Instead, He said to the people standing there, "You unwrap him."

God is calling each of us to knock at the door of someone who is bound in strips of linen—unable to walk out of their tomb that keeps them shrouded in darkness—while the Son waits patiently to cast His light abroad in their heart. Rather, we stay bound by things that may have tortured us, even since childhood. "Come forth, my child." Jesus came to set the captives free.

> Amazing grace, how sweet the sound,
> that saved a wretch like me.
> I once was lost but now I'm found,
> was blind, but now I see.

> —John Newton

How amazing is His grace for you and me! We cannot begin to comprehend the vastness of His love. Romans 8:38–39 says, "For I am convinced that neither death nor life, neither angels nor demons, neither the present nor the future, nor any powers, neither height nor depth, nor anything else in all creation, will be able to separate us from the love of God that is in Christ Jesus our Lord."

This world cannot contain the love of Jesus. Even those who are yet to answer the door to their hearts are loved with a love that summons them to the One who giveth more grace.

> He giveth more grace when the burdens grow
>   greater;
> He sendeth more strength when the labors increase.
> To added affliction, He addeth His mercy;
> To multiplied trials, His multiplied peace.
> His love has no limit, His grace has no measure;

His power has no boundary known unto men.
For out of His infinite riches in Jesus;
He giveth, and giveth, and giveth again!

—Annie Johnson Flint

Dear friend, allow Jesus to grant you provisions out of the richness of His storehouse. His fields are ripe unto harvest. His supply is never-ending. His resources are vast beyond measure. Receive all that He has for you in this life and the next. His grace is yours in abundance should you choose to accept it as a gift from on high.

"Grace and peace to you from Him Who is, and Who was, and Who is to come" (Revelation 1:4). "'I am the Alpha and Omega,' says the Lord God, 'Who is, and Who was, and Who is to come, the Almighty'" (verse 8). The grace of the Lord Jesus be with God's people. Amen.

Grace, grace, God's grace,
coming down from the Father above.
Sweep over my spirit forever I pray,
in fathomless billows of love.

—Don Moen

LONELINESS

"Jesus often withdrew to lonely places and prayed" (Luke 5:16).

It is well understood that all of us have experienced loneliness at one time or another in our lives. In fact, it is possible to feel as lonely in a crowded mall or in a church sanctuary, as it is in our own homes secluded from the world. Loneliness can eat away at our spirits, causing even more feelings of desolation and perhaps feelings of contempt for ourselves. We think something is wrong with us if others do not ring our doorbells while we sit in front of our televisions, hunkered down in our beds to evade the friendliness which might make us rise up and feel part of our community.

Perhaps we are feeling lonely because we are afraid to be with other people or because other people have not reached out to us. We need to let go of the loneliness that fills our empty stomachs and makes us feel isolated from mankind. Loneliness makes us feel unwanted or uncared for. It can eat at the very fiber of our soul. We might ask ourselves what is wrong with us when we so long for companionship that our hearts ache with its lack.

Are you alone in your misery? In your marriage? In life? Aloneness can be debilitating. It can rob you of the essence of living. How can you reconnect with others? What would give you the desire to risk again, to surrender yourself to that which you fear, to abandon that which has you bound like the grip of a vice?

God created us to be one with Him and with each other. He does not want us to live isolated from others or from ourselves. The enemy of our souls seeks to isolate us from persons or things that give us a sense of belonging.

Isolation can be an enemy that makes us feel like we have no worth or value. Rather than feelings of belonging, we feel like exiles that are unwelcome—leaving us feeling lonely. However, even though loneliness can make us feel uncomfortable, God can use it for our good if we seek Him and help other sojourners in our world feel comfortable.

It is not necessary to even ask if you have felt lonely at times. Can you think of what might be the cause of your loneliness? Is it because you are afraid to be with other people or because other people have not reached out to you? What could remedy your situation? Often we expect others to meet our needs, when our lives would be more fruitful if we reached out and ministered to them.

Who do you need to reach out to today? In doing so, might you feel more connected to those you avoid and become a part of the companionship that is available to you, waiting for you to come and sup with them? Come, dear one, and let go of the loneliness that fills your empty stomach and makes you feel isolated from mankind. Ask God to fill the lonely places in your life. He is waiting for you.

Loneliness is modern-day leprosy,
and people do not want others to know.

—Mother Teresa

LAMENT

Jesus cried out in a loud voice,
"Eli, Eli, lema sabachthani?"
(which means)
"My God, My God, why have You forsaken Me?"
(Matthew 27:46)

Have you ever cried out from the depths of your soul, "My God, my God, where are You?" Have you ever hungered for His presence more than food which can satisfy only your body while your spirit is withering? Do you feel like you are wandering in a parched desert that is devouring all your energy?

From King David in the Old Testament to King Jesus in the New, men of all ages have yearned for God's manifest presence in their lives by lamenting His seeming absence. Nearly one-half of Psalms consist of David's laments. Are you in the valley of lament, trying to touch the hem of Jesus' garment? The Bible describes Him as a *Man of Sorrows;* familiar with suffering.

It is common for Christians to feel like we should be victorious, but tears are an expression of lament which penetrate the depth of human emotion. That's what Jesus experienced in the Garden of Gethsemane as He beseeched His Father.

Laments can only be entered by our High Priest expressed with blood, sweat, and tears. The answer to all our laments is the presence of God with us, manifested in Scripture with, "I will never leave you nor forsake you" (Hebrews 13:5). Even in the midst of our most profound despair, God is ever-present.

Lament is not letting go of our faith, but clinging to it with a grasp that will not let go. It leads us to praise the One who hears our desperate cries and soothes our aching hearts. There, we can receive God's forgiveness and be cleansed for our journey. Learn the language of lament and allow the Healer to make you *broken unto wholeness.*

Evil and pain will not have the last word.
The valley of the shadow of death is not our final destination.

—Michael Jenkins

WOUNDED SOUL

Are you discouraged? Do you feel like life is too hard? Do you feel like giving up? Good news awaits you!

God's Son, Jesus, came to earth, was crucified, and was taken up into heaven where He sits at the right hand of His Father, pleading for you and me that we might be set free from the chains of bondage that make us slaves to sin.

Sin separates us from God. Jesus' shed blood on Calvary cleanses us. He died to make a way for us to His Father Who is waiting with open arms to receive us when we ask and receive the Son into our hearts. Jesus is the Way!

> I am the Way and the Truth and the Life.
> No one comes to the Father, but through Me.
> (John 14:6)

I care about the pain you are experiencing, dear one, and Jesus cares, too. He gave His life that you and I might be made whole. He is waiting to receive you into His loving arms. Please don't resist Him. He longs to hold you and ease your pain.

We all sin and fall short of God's glory (Romans 3:23). But God the Father sacrificed His Son Jesus that we might be made right with Him. Don't let Jesus have died in vain for you. He paid the ultimate price for your release from the shackles that bind you.

> If we claim to be without sin,
> we deceive ourselves and the truth is not in us.
> If we confess our sins,
> He is faithful and just and will forgive our sins

and purify us from all unrighteousness.
(1 John 1:8–9)

Let today be a turning point in the pain you have been living in. You don't need to carry your burden any longer. Jesus is waiting to take it from you, if you will just lay it at the foot of His cross. Jesus has already paid your price. Give it to Him and be set free this day.

> To Him who sits on the throne (God the Father)
> and to the Lamb (Jesus, the Son He sacrificed
>   for us)
> be praise and honor and glory and power
> forever and ever! Amen.
> (Revelation 5:13–14)

Invite the Lamb into your Heart
so He can be the Shepherd of your Life.

DISAPPOINTMENT

Disappointment is the gap between
expectations and reality.

—John Maxwell

Are you disappointed with yourself? Are you disappointed with life? Disappointment travels down many avenues. Sometimes it can feel like the whole world is against us. We can feel like our life is flashing before us, and we regret all those we have hurt and all the things left undone. Everything we do seems to go wrong which makes us frustrated and like life is too hard. We might even be tempted to look for an escape.

Hopelessness can feel like a snake has slithered into our lives and wrapped its coils around us until we struggle to get our very breath. We can feel stuck in a cesspool of slimy muck and mire that is pulling us down. We feel like we will never be able to get our heads above the murky water that is trying to drown us in the disdain we feel for ourselves.

God is well aware of our struggles, my friend. He desires to help us through the tests and trials we face. Philip Yancey writes in *Disappointment with God*, "One bold message in the book of Job is that you can say anything to God. Throw at Him, your grief, your anger, your doubt, your bitterness, your betrayal, your disappointment—He can absorb them all."[3] We only need to lean on Him and let the breathings of His Holy Spirit envelop us and work in us to become all He designed us to be.

---

3   Philip Yancey, *Disappointment with God* (Zondervan, 1988)

Depression can also overshadow us until we think we might never see the light of day. Its dark cloud hovers over us, shutting out any hope we might have for the future. A year after accepting the Lord over four decades ago, I felt as if my world was shattered, along with my very being. The turmoil in my gut cut through all other emotions, making me feel isolated from my beloved husband, young children, and those I held dear.

Anguish tormented my mind until I felt as if I were literally going crazy. Only the love and support of my husband saw me through to the other side of that dark valley.

I was unable to feel the presence of the One who gave His life that I might have eternal life with Him and abundant life here on earth. Feeling separated from my newfound Savior left me feeling hopeless and scared. I felt doomed to living my life in a pit of despair and earnestly wanted to escape the terrible emptiness that was consuming me. How could Jesus abandon me when I was still learning to walk by faith? Would I ever be free of this horrible disease that was gnawing in my stomach, in my soul?

Later, a wise friend shared that God sometimes leaves us feeling abandoned because He wants our faith to develop so that we can grow strong in Him. Second Corinthians 12:10 says, "For when we are weak, then we are strong." Our Lord desires that we walk uprightly and not toddle around as immature children. In the King James Version, Proverbs 22:6 says, "Train a child in the way he should go." That is precisely what our heavenly Father is doing in our lives. We are His children, but His plan is that we be trained in His way that will be the best way.

Are you wandering down a blind alley, looking to find your way? Sometimes God uses what feels like detours to us to put us on the path He designed for us to walk. Detours can actually be roads to blessings. An unknown author wrote, "A bend in the road is not the end of the road, unless you fail to make the turn." Recording artist Sara Groves said, "It is one thing to see someone taking the road less traveled, and then another to see someone forging their own road."

Are you forging a road that will lead you down the straight and narrow? Roads have many twists and turns and bumps along the way.

They can take us to the destination we had planned or they can take us somewhere we don't want to go, and we might have to backtrack to find our way.

Following is a quote by Joyce Meyers, "Disappointment comes from unmet expectations." Sometimes we can have our sights set too high—beyond that which we are able to reach. Expectations can be noble goals, but they must be within reason.

Disappointment can bring discouragement into our lives that can be difficult to overcome. Don't let the spirit of discouragement consume you, my friend, lest the enemy of your soul rob you of God's best.

God longs to encourage us so that we can rise above our disappointments, if we will but allow Him to use them as stepping stones to reach heights we never envisioned.

Our lives should not be defined by things we are unable to achieve but, by those things that set our feet on higher ground, so that we can be an encouragement to others who are downtrodden and feeling discouraged. Allow disappointments to be avenues of growth in your life. The only way our faith will grow is if God puts us in a place where we have to use it. The only way we can serve our God freely is as we allow Him to make us...

Broken unto Wholeness.

PAIN AND SUFFERING

"The purpose of suffering is to bring us to a place of surrender."

Are you suffering, my friend? Do you feel wracked with pain—both emotionally and physically—until life has become burdensome? Has a snake slithered under the backdoor of your life and entangled itself around every nerve in your body? Has its venom poisoned your thoughts until the very essence of your being feels wearisome? Do you wish the pain would just stop so you can move on with your life? You may be asking with Jeremiah, "Why is my pain unending?" (15:18).

What do you think God could be trying to teach you? It has been said that the greatest lessons in life come from suffering. Are you learning the lesson well or are your emotions blocking the pathway to healing? Experience is the hardest teacher because it gives you tests before it gives you lessons.

We must remember that sometimes Jesus comes in the midst of our pain rather than delivering us from it. E. H. Chapin said, "Out of suffering have emerged the strongest souls; the most massive characters are seamed with scars."

Are your wounds infected with self-loathing while you blame others for your brokenness? Did you know God can use your brokenness to make you whole? But until we surrender ourselves to whatever it is that has us caught in the grips of defeat, we will stay in the ruins of our own destruction.

Jesus came that we might conquer those things that have us bound in the grave clothes of our own making. We need to rip out the seams that are taut from years of pulling and stretching before the fabric of our lives is torn beyond repair.

Our Lord came to set us free. He desires to heal the broken-hearted, to bind up the bruised. Though He may seem far away, He is as close as we will allow Him to be. He is waiting to soothe our broken spirits and comfort our contrite hearts. "The sacrifices of God are a broken spirit; a broken and contrite heart" (Psalm 51:17 KJV). He came to mold us from being *broken unto wholeness*.

Do not cast Him aside, dear one. Your life and well-being hang in the balance. The Name of Jesus is your salvation. Let Him lift you out of the miry clay and put your feet on a firm foundation. He is the Rock that will anchor you against the storms of life. His arms will hold you secure when your world is falling apart. He is able to put the broken pieces of your life together and give you purpose and meaning for living.

The enemy of our souls would tell us we do not have value or worth in this world. But he is a liar! He came to steal and kill and destroy (John 10:10). We must rise above those things that would bring us to the brink of despair. We must not allow he who is evil to defeat us and make us feel unworthy. God is truth, and Satan is a liar!

For those of us who struggle with our personhood—the very people God created us to be—it is likely we are buying into the lies of the enemy of our souls and coming up short. Our emotional bank accounts are bankrupt. How long will we allow ourselves to be deceived by the messenger of Satan and allow him to torment us? (2 Corinthians 12:7).

God did not create us to be placed on the rubbish heap of bruised and battered self-images. He created us in His image. We are loved and esteemed in His sight. He has a wonderful plan for our lives; plans to give us hope and a future (Jeremiah 29:11).

Author Larry Crabb says, "The basic personal need of each person is to regard himself as a worthwhile human being." God created us for a purpose, and we must strive to be obedient to that which He has called us. Give God the pieces of your life, and He will give you the peace of Christ.

> Suffer not who you were,
> but celebrate who you are.

—Steven Erickson

Have you ever experienced a hurricane with the velocity of Katrina sweep through your home, wiping away every personal belonging you owned? Have you had a tsunami decimate not only your bungalow but the very land it inhabited? Has a fire ignited your home and destroyed its contents into tinder? Have you been raped in your soul in a way that bruised your personhood and left you feeling scarred for life?

There are so many tragedies in this world. Souls lie wounded everywhere—some in gutters, some in filth-ridden shelters, and some sleeping in cardboard boxes. Or some at the hands of an assault rifle shot by a deranged person in need of being made...

Broken unto Wholeness.

THE STORM WILL PASS

Exodus 5:1, 17–18, 22–23 paraphrased:

Moses appealed to Pharaoh to let the people go, but instead he multiplied their workload and the situation went from bad to horrible. Moses found it hard to believe that a glorious exodus could be just around the corner.

The plans of the Lord were not being frustrated, however. Before conditions would get better for His children, God tested them by allowing their suffering to increase.

Even when we are obedient to the Lord, the skies of adversity may not always clear immediately. Circumstances may get worse before they improve. But praise be to God, His grace will sustain us and *the storm will pass!*

Amen and Amen!

A MESSAGE OF ENCOURAGEMENT

The Oak Tree

A mighty wind blew night and day.
It stole the oak tree's leaves away.
Then snapped its boughs and pulled its bark,
Until the oak was tired and stark.
But still the oak tree held its ground,
While other trees fell all around.
The weary wind gave up and spoke,
"How can you still be standing, Oak?"
The oak tree said, "I know that you
Can break each branch of mine in two,
Carry every leaf away,
Shake my limbs, and make me sway.
But I have roots stretched in the earth,
Growing stronger since my birth.
You'll never touch them, for, you see,
They are the deepest part of me.
Until today, I wasn't sure
Of just how much I could endure.
But now I've found, with thanks to you,
I'm stronger than I ever knew."

Hallmark Cares

"For no one can lay any foundation other than
the one already laid, which is Jesus Christ"
(1 Corinthians 3:11).

CARING AND COMPASSION

Be kind and compassionate to one another, forgiving each other, just as in Christ God forgave you. (Ephesians 4:32)

What has God entrusted to your care? Are you being a good steward of His provision? Are you nurturing hurting souls as He nourishes your spirit? Jesus tells us in John 21:15, "Feed My lambs."

Caring is like a cup of cold water on a scorching day in midsummer. It runs through our spirits and quenches our dry, thirsty souls. But like the Living Water in John chapter four, Jesus permeates our beings with His presence that shall never run dry.

Our God is full of compassion. Second Corinthians 1:3 tells us, "He is the Father of compassion." His mercies are new every morning. When darkness invades our souls, His caring arms soothe our spirits until joy returns again.

He protects us, sustains us, and grants us His unfailing love out of the richness of Who He is. He is love, and He loves us! How blessed we are to have the infilling of His Spirit minister to us in our darkest hours. His presence—manifest in our earthly vessels—comforts us and brings us peace.

He is our refuge in times of trouble. On whom else could we rely? Psalm 142:4 says, "Look to my right and see; no one is concerned for me. I have no refuge; no one cares for my life." God is our only source. He tells us to cast our cares on Him. No one else can care for us like the One who lives in us. His indwelling Spirit is a solace when the world around us races until we cannot catch our breath.

"Cast your cares on the Lord because He cares for you" (1 Peter 5:7). Almighty God cares for me and He cares for you.

"God, who is full of compassion, redeems our lives from the pit and crowns us with His love and compassion" (Psalm 103:4). How blessed we are to be clothed in robes of righteousness by the One and only righteous One! The King who reigns on high! The Messiah! Yahweh!

According to Your great compassion, dear Lord, receive our praise. Great are You, Holy God, and most worthy of praise! We, who are unworthy, are honored to be called to "live a life worthy of Your calling" (Ephesians 4:1).

Colossians 3:12 tells us, "As God's chosen people, holy and dearly loved, clothe yourselves with compassion, kindness, humility, gentleness and patience."

We are chosen of God! We who fall short of His glory daily. We who sin against our brothers and sisters, our mothers and fathers, our sons and daughters. "Forgive us, Lord." In the words of Your Son, Jesus, "Father, forgive them, for they do not know what they are doing" (Luke 23:24a).

Our eyes are covered with a film that dims our vision. Open our eyes, Lord, that we might see You clearly. Help us capture the essence of Your beauty that will make our sight brighter. We know Your beauty is awesome to behold—full of grandeur and splendor. We want to see You, Jesus.

> Open my eyes, Lord;
> I want to see Jesus.
> To reach out and touch Him;
> To show Him I love Him.
>
> Open my ears, Lord;
> and help me to listen.
> Open my eyes, Lord;
> I want to see Jesus.

> —Robert Cull

My heart grieves for you, dear one. I care for you and your pain. I want to be there for you. Please don't shut me out. God cares for you, too. Please don't shut Him out.

He has a plan for your life. Let Him show you. Let Him love you. Let Him hold you in His arms. He longs to touch your heart with His.

Let His grace bind up your wounds. His Word tells us, "He is the Way, the Truth, and the Life" (John 14:6). He cares for you and your life. Give Him your all and let Him make you *broken unto wholeness*. Don't let Him have died in vain for you.

He is the Rock that holds firm. He is your Rock. Cast your cares on Him. Be healed in His Name for His sake and yours. So be it!

GOD CARES

Someone once asked the question, "Who cares?" and God answered, "I care." You may be asking that question now in your hour of trial. "Who cares? Does anyone care about me in my present need?"

Many years ago, David, the psalmist, expressed a similar feeling, "Look to my right and see; no one is concerned for me. I have no refuge; no one cares for my life" (Psalm 142:4).

But there is good news! There is One who cares about you and wants to be your closest friend. Man may fail you when the going is hard, but God never fails those who put their trust in Him. The apostle Peter wrote, "Cast all your anxiety on Him because He cares for you" (1 Peter 5:7). Whatever your burden may be at this hour, will you not let God bear it? He has proved to countless thousands through the years to be...

A loving Friend.

The Bible tells us that "a friend loves at all times, and a brother is born for adversity" (Proverbs 17:17). God is not unaware of your burden. His love reaches out to you at this moment. The Word of God speaks of the love of God in these words, "This is love: not that we loved God, but that He loved us and sent His Son as an atoning sacrifice for our sins" (1 John 4:10).

God has permitted this trial to come into your life so that you might turn to Him and receive His love in Christ. It has been said, "God often digs wells of joy with the spade of sorrow." God's wonderful love in Christ can change a dark outlook to a bright one in times of trial. His love can chase away the shadows of gloom and turn your night into day.

Dear one, I know your sorrows.
Your every trial I share.
I know how much you are tested.
And what is more—I care.
God has also proved Himself to be...
A lasting Friend.

God's love and care for you is unchangeable. You can depend upon His faithfulness to give you strength to meet each new day with its trials and burdens. "Your strength will equal your days" (Deuteronomy 33:25).

The story is told of a hardworking man who fell on difficult days. Through no fault of his own, he lost his own health and savings, and at last his family faced ruin. A rich man heard of his plight and sent him an envelope of money with a note attached which read, *More to follow.* After a few days, another envelope arrived with a gift and a note attached with a message, *More to follow.* For many days and weeks, the family received such help—always with the cheering message, *More to follow*—until the man and his family were back on their feet.

So it is with God's care. He supplies sufficient strength and grace for present needs, and there is always the cheering assurance for each new day: "*More to follow.*"

Who cares about you in your present need? God cares. His love for you was supremely seen when Christ died for you. "Greater love has no one than this, that one lay down his life for his friends" (John 15:13). Will you not let God prove to be a loving and lasting friend to you?

"Cast your cares on the Lord and He will
sustain you" (Psalm 55:22).

FORGIVENESS

> For if you forgive other people when they sin
> against you, your Heavenly Father will also for-
> give you. But if you do not forgive others their
> sins, your Father will not forgive your sins.
> (Matthew 6:14–15)

Forgiveness can be harder to come by than a two-dollar bill. It eludes us like a rainbow on a cloudy day. Forgiveness is a gift—more to ourselves than the person who has trespassed against us. Our willingness to let go of things that would trap us as an oyster shell will bring us a sense of freedom that soothes our hearts and sets us free from the tentacles that ensnare us.

Unforgiveness, on the other hand, keeps us bound by things over which we may have no control. Perhaps those who have committed an offense against us are not even aware and go about living their lives happily ever after.

As a new Christian, I desperately wanted the Lord to wipe my slate clean so that I could walk forth a new creature in Christ. One day—in deep concentration of spirit—I uttered to the Lord, "Heal my memories and I will forgive my parents." And in the depths of my innermost being, I heard these words from the One who is our Healer, "Forgive your parents, and I will heal your memories."

Wow! That put the ball back in my court. Sometimes we try to avoid our responsibility in situations where our feelings are hurt. We try to get even by playing the blame game, thinking that will make things right while it sets up a barrier that separates us from our Lord. No matter how fast we run, we cannot escape the horror of our unrighteousness.

Scripture says we are to forgive our brother as we forgive our-selves. Do you struggle with unforgiveness? Against your brother or against yourself? The Word of God tells us if we don't forgive, we will not be forgiven.

> If you forgive anyone, I also forgive.
> And what I have forgiven—
> If there is anything to forgive—
> I have forgiven in the sight of Christ.
> (2 Corinthians 2:10)

ABYSS TO REDEMPTION

> For He has rescued us from the dominion of darkness and brought us into the kingdom of the Son He loves, in whom we have redemption, the forgiveness of sins. (Colossians 1:13–14)

Have you ever plunged or leapt headlong into an abyss so deep you might never have recovered, except for God's redeeming grace? Do you feel like you are alone in your pain, your agony too great to bear? God is waiting for you on the other side, my friend, to rescue you from the dominion of darkness that looms in your mind.

Our heavenly Father is so merciful and kind, full of love and unmerited favor. Nothing you have done can keep you from His amazing grace. He awaits you with outstretched arms. He is able to put the pieces of your life together again and, through the shed blood of His Son, He is able to redeem your life into more than you ever dreamed possible. He is able to make you *broken unto wholeness.*

Our suffering can bring us to a place of surrender like nothing else can. We don't have the combination to the lock that imprisons us in anguish and grief, but God does. He knows what each one of us needs personally and what can give our lives purpose and meaning and direction for living. Be assured He longs to do that for you, friend.

In *The Search for Significance*, Robert McGee writes, "When we find that we perceive our lives as having no value, purpose or significance, we become miserable."[4] To those of us who have experienced

---

4   Robert S. McGee, *Search for Significance* (Nashville, Tennessee: W Publishing Group, a Division of Thomas Nelson, Inc. 2003).

that perception, we understand the reality of that statement. Some people even lose their desire to live.

Have you ever sunk so low you simply wanted to die to alleviate the pain you were feeling? Did your life seem so futile you lost all hope? In Psalm 55:4–5, David writes of his despair, "My heart is in anguish within me; the terrors of death assail me. Fear and trembling have beset me; horror has overwhelmed me." Are you able to relate to the one God called *a man after My own heart?*

There is hope for us, my friend. We are not alone in the torment of our souls. We just need to seek the One who knows us better than we know ourselves. He has a plan for each one of us that will bring us not only fulfillment but also joy unspeakable. Please don't give up on yourself but, even more importantly, don't give up on your Creator.

His Word tells us He holds us in the palms of His hands (Isaiah 49:16). No matter how bleak life feels, His grace is greater still. He has a plan for your life that cannot be thwarted by you or the enemy of your soul.

I speak from personal experience, dear wounded soul. My words are not hollow nor the deep caring I feel for you in my heart. I can relate to your pain with heartfelt empathy. And I want to assure you, God can and will redeem your life from the pit you have dug for yourself, if you will but trust Him.

Listen to what His Word tells us when things seem overwhelming and impossible for us, "For nothing is impossible with God" (Luke 1:37). Nothing, absolutely nothing!

"Cast all your anxiety on Him because He cares for you" (1 Peter 5:7).

His miracle-working power is awaiting your permission to release you from the prison that holds you captive. He desires to set you free from those things that ensnare you. His supernatural grace is able to free you from all that binds you. He can and wants to "redeem your life from the pit" (Psalms 103:4).

Luke 4:17–19 says, "The scroll of the prophet Isaiah was handed to Jesus. Unrolling it, He found the place where it is written: 'The Spirit of the Lord is on Me, because He has anointed Me to preach good news to the poor. He has sent Me to proclaim freedom for the prisoners and recovery of sight for the blind, to release the oppressed, to proclaim the year of the Lord's favor.'" Won't you allow His proclamation to become real in your heart and life?

He died to set you free, friend. He longs to open your prison gates so that you might come forth, as Lazarus did. The following excerpt from Keith Miller and Bruce Larson's *The Passionate People* makes my point:

"When Jesus stood at the tomb of Lazarus and called his name, he walked out of the grave alive. This was miraculous. But all Lazarus could say, with gritted teeth, was 'Hallelujah!' He was alive but he was totally bound in grave clothes. And the surprising thing is that Jesus never got Lazarus out of the grave clothes, according to the Scriptures. What Jesus did, instead, was turn to the people standing around Lazarus and say, 'You unwrap him.'"[5]

I believe that one of the greatest ways we have to uncover hidden resources is to be in a group we have given permission to unwrap us. I think this is where many of us in the church are. We have been brought to life wrapped in the grave clothes of other people's expectations of us—sometimes from childhood. We have been wrapped in the grave clothes of our fears of disappointing other people. We have been afraid that our own hopes and dreams and inner resources would not be worthy to obtain the love we feel we must have. Then we can come out and use the hands and feet and the gifts God has given us. Many of these gifts may have become bound inside us for years by our own brokenness and lostness and that of the people around us. For all of us have somewhere hidden inside us something of the creative life Christ has promised to use in loving the world.

Are you living in isolation, dear one? It is such a lonely place to exist—often paralyzing you in your woundedness. It is not God's will for you to live out your days sequestered from those who could pour the balm of Gilead into your hurting soul and bind up your wounds with the compassion of Jesus.

---

[5] Keith Miller & Bruce Larson, *The Passionate People*, (Waco, TX: Word Inc. 1979)

If you are possibly contemplating putting your life on the threshold of eternity, please reconsider! Even though we walk through the valley of the shadow of death, He is with us. When things seem absolutely hopeless in our lives, the One who is hope can bring life back to us anew. His vision is much more clear than ours. The future He has in store for us is bright with promise because He is Lord, and "He came that we may have life, and have it to the full" (John 10:10).

Hold on, my child! His plan for your life is not yet fulfilled. Reach out and take the hand of someone who cares about you more deeply than you know. No matter what you may have been told in the past, you are a valuable person with worth and potential. Do not let the enemy of your soul deceive you into believing your life is futile and that the world would be better off without you. The world would be minus the only you there can ever be, and that would be a loss that could never be replaced.

God created you with a purpose in mind, and His mind says you are loved and wanted on earth. "For God so loved the world that He gave His one and only Son, that whoever believes in Him shall not perish but have eternal life" (John 3:16). Remember, to the world you are one person, but to the One you are the world. Live for Him.

HEALER

"I am God your Healer" (Exodus 15:26).

Has pain ever drenched you like rain? Has a downpour soaked you to your core with its cold, clammy sensation or has it simply drizzled over the residue in your life like a soft summer shower that washes away the dust from yesterday?

Pain can certainly take a toll on our lives, not only physically but emotionally, as well. It can consume every morsel of that which we are seeking to achieve. It can divert and distract us from the calling of God on our lives.

Detours on life's journey can put us on paths of destruction if we don't keep our eyes on Jesus as we travel His pathway. Sinkholes can entrap us until we feel like we have fallen into a pit that requires all of our strength and energy to find our way out. Pain can be an enemy that encroaches on our lives, but it can also make us aware of things in our lives that are out of balance and in need of alignment to keep us from toppling over.

We must learn how to counteract its sometimes vicious attack on our bodies and emotions. It can be very difficult to overcome. Its clutch can hinder us from moving forward. We might hobble along for months or even years, until relief settles over us like a healing balm. Encouragement restores the ache that has besieged us to the point of giving out or giving in. Discouragement has lost the battle, and we march forth victorious over its looming cloud. Sunshine shines through our darkness to reveal the Light of the world Who we desperately sought while we felt crippled and broken.

God is the Healer of the brokenhearted and binds up our wounds (Psalm 147:3). He inspires us to keep walking toward wholeness. His Word promises us that He will wipe away our tears and help us to continue on the road to a bright tomorrow, if we do not let yesterday's failure overtake our present which could defeat tomorrow's victory.

Praise be to the One who holds us in the palms of His hands and sets our feet on the Rock. Resting in His arms can be an avenue the Lord uses to help us find our way, giving us hope for the dawning of a new day. Rather than allowing ourselves to be scourged by the enemy of our souls—with the Lord in our lives—we can rise above the muck and mire that so easily besets us. We must allow Jesus to touch us and grant us a destiny of promise and abundant living. We must allow Him to make us *broken unto wholeness*. So be it, Lord Jesus!

ALPHA AND OMEGA

I am the Alpha and Omega, the First and the Last,
the Beginning and the End. (Revelation 22:13)

Do you sometimes feel at the end of yourself? Do you feel like you're going down a road that has no destination? Do you feel like the world has passed you by? My friend, the world is only rotating on its axis. Do not fear; it shall come around again.

God has a wonderful plan for your life, and He has not abandoned you. His Word says, "He will never leave you nor forsake you" (Joshua 1:5; Hebrews 13:5). He is as close as your very breath. He is breathing His lifeblood into you at this very moment.

Receive all that He is offering you. Don't let a morsel fall from your plate. His crumbs are more delectable than a seven-course meal, including dessert. You are not at the end; you are only at the beginning of all He has for you.

What can seem like the end in someone's life may very well be the beginning of a chapter yet to be written. Hang on to the Author and Finisher of your faith. His Name is Jesus.

What we call the beginning, is often the end.
And to make an end, is to make a beginning.
The end is where we start from.

—Maxie Dunnam,
Dancing At My Funeral

When we get to the end of ourselves,
we have nothing left—
But God.

—Michael Card,
A Sacred Sorrow

REFLECTIVE
MEDITATIONS

"If anything is excellent or praiseworthy, think about such things"
(Philippians 4:8).

BUT GOD

When we have nothing left but God, we discover
that God is enough.

I want to share about a *miracle* God performed in my life. The theme of my testimony is: But God. On January 16, 2009, I had arthroscopic surgery on my left shoulder as a result of our car accident nearly three years earlier. The surgery went well, and I went home expecting a full recovery. However, I was having difficulty regaining my strength, and four days later, I collapsed in Gary's (my husband) arms.

He immediately called 911, and I was rushed to the hospital where I spent the next six hours in Emergency. I'm told a CAT scan was done of my brain to make sure I had not had a stroke. A couple of hours later, the technicians did a CAT scan of my chest and it was determined that both my lungs were full of blood clots. I spent the next five days in the hospital. Several medical people told me, "If it had not been for Gary's swift action, I probably would not have survived." However, the *miracle* is that I am alive! But God.

Now I'd like to share with you *the rest of the story.* Gary and I graduated from high school together and celebrated our fifty-fifth wedding anniversary last June. He has always supported me and fulfilled Ephesians 5:25, "Husbands, love your wives, just as Christ loved the church, and gave Himself up for her."

Through this time, as I stood on the threshold of eternity, Gary's love and caring were never more evident. Both in the hospital and upon my return home, he slept by my bedside, praying God would save my life. And I believe I am alive today: But for God and Gary.

We sometimes take our spouses—and life itself—for granted. As I lay on the hospital bed, a clock on the wall ticked constantly. And as the days went by, I realized that we never know—from one tick to the next tock—when our life will come to an end.

I feel blessed and humbled, knowing in my heart it was: But God. Jesus saved my soul, but God used Gary to save my life. I am indebted to both.

A phrase that has been etched on my heart during this time is: "When we get to the end of ourselves, we have nothing left. But God."

PRAYER

"If you believe, you will receive whatever you ask
for in prayer" (Matthew 21:22).

Prayer is communication with God, not just our words but also
our hearts. It is connecting with the person we are praying for, as
well as the One we are praying to. It is spiritual communion with
our Lord. It is not just about praying for the person but praying
with them, agreeing together for their request. Matthew 18:19 says,
"Again, I tell you that if two of you on earth agree about anything
you ask for, it will be done for you by My Father in heaven."

We need to focus not only on the need of the person we are
praying for, but also on the Person we are praying to. How we con-
nect with someone will long be remembered after our words are forgotten. As John Bunyan said, "In prayer, it is better to have a heart
without words than words without a heart."

Listening is crucial to connecting with those we are praying for.
We can't hear if we don't listen to the Holy Spirit. He is all-knowing.
He knows not only the need, but He also knows the answer. We will
reap results if we allow Him to answer as we pray. Miracles happen as
we wait on Him. Being specific shows our intent while confidently
expecting God to act.

Prayer is also about caring—when a person is going away from
us as much or more as when they are coming toward us. Follow-up
is very important, as well. Some of my best friends are people I have
prayed for. What we are called to do is of utmost importance that we
cannot take lightly. It is an honor to be used by the Lord. We must
be careful to give Him the glory that is His!

Another essential ingredient is faith. In Matthew 17:20, Jesus said unto the disciples, "I tell you the truth, if you have faith as small as a mustard seed, you can say to this mountain, 'Move from here to there' and it will move. Nothing will be impossible for you."

In *The Battle Plan for Prayer*, Stephen and Alex Kendrick wrote the following, "King David worshipped, as you can worship, by saying to the Lord, 'You satisfy me as with rich food; my mouth will praise You with joyful lips' (Psalm 63:5 HCSB). Before going to bed at night, he looked into God's face as his last thought of the day, saying, 'When I awake, I will be satisfied with Your presence' (Psalm 17:15 HCSB). He wanted God to be his first thought and first prayer in the morning as well."

The Word can guide your prayers of *adoration*: "Yours, O Lord is the greatness and the power and the glory and the victory and the majesty... You rule over all, and in Your hand is power and might" (1 Chronicles 29:11–12).

Your prayers of *confession*: "Create in me a clean heart, O God, and renew a steadfast spirit within me... Restore to me the joy of Your salvation and sustain me with a willing spirit" (Psalm 51:10, 12).

Your prayers of *thanksgiving*: "Give thanks to the Lord, for He is good; for His loving kindness is everlasting... I shall give thanks to You, for You have answered me, and You have become my salvation" (Psalm 118:1, 21).

Your prayers of *supplication*: "O Lord of hosts, hear my prayer... No good thing does He withhold from those who walk uprightly" (Psalm 84:8, 11).[6]

We are all familiar with James 5:16 (KJV), "The effectual fervent prayer of a righteous man availeth much." But I truly believe that in order to be scripturally correct, we must pray in the Name of Jesus. John 14:13–14 tells us, "And I will do whatever you ask in My Name, so that the Father may be glorified in the Son. You may ask me for anything in My Name, and I will do it."

---

[6]   Stephen & Alex Kendrick, *The Battle Plan for Prayer*, (B&H Publishing Group, 2015)

"For where two or three come together in My Name, there I am with them" (Matthew 18:20).

Prayer occupied a place of singular importance in Jesus' own life and teaching. In times of decision and crisis, even He gave Himself to prayer.

There is a story behind the old hymn, "Let the Lower Lights Be Burning." It refers to a shipwreck caused when the harbor lights were not on, even though the lighthouse tower light was on. The composer saw Christ as the lighthouse, and Christians as the harbor lights.

P.P. Bliss wrote, "Trim your feeble lamp, my brother; some poor sailor tempest tossed. Trying now to make the harbor; in the darkness may be lost."

We know Jesus is the Light, but we are like the harbor lights praying for those who may be trying to make the harbor. Thus, we need to stay sensitive to storm-tossed people.

"God will carry you through the storm" (Isaiah 43:2).

The Lord's Prayer

> Our Father in heaven,
> hallowed be Your Name,
> Your Kingdom come, Your will be done,
> on earth as it is in heaven.
> Give us today our daily bread. And forgive us our sins,
> as we also have forgiven those who have sinned
> against us.
> And lead us not into temptation,
> but deliver us from the evil one.
> For Yours is the Kingdom and the power and the
> glory forever.
> Amen.

Teaching about Prayer

Jesus said, "This is how you should pray:
Father, may Your Name be kept holy.
May Your Kingdom come soon.
Give us each day the food we need,
and forgive us our sins,
as we forgive those who sin against us.
And don't let us yield to temptation."
(Luke 11:2–4 NLT)

Prayer of St. Francis of Assisi

Lord,
Make me an instrument of Your peace;
Where there is hatred, let me sow love;
Where there is injury, pardon;
Where there is doubt, faith;
Where there is despair, hope;
Where there is darkness, light;
Where there is sadness, joy.

O Divine Master,
Grant that I may not so much
seek to be consoled as to console;
To be understood as to understand;
To be loved as to love.

For it is in giving that we receive.
It is in pardoning that we are pardoned.
It is in dying that we are born to eternal life.

LISTEN

"Listen to His voice and hold fast to Him"
(Deuteronomy 30:20).

Have you listened to the voice of God? Do you listen to what He is telling you to do? Is He speaking to you at this moment? Will you be obedient to the sound of His voice? John 10:27 says, "My sheep listen to My voice; I know them and they follow Me." Jesus tells us to listen to the voice of God.

> For who listens to us in all the world
> Whether he be friend or teacher, brother or father or
> Mother, sister or neighbor, son or ruler, or
> Servant? Does he listen, our advocate, or our
> Husbands or wives, those who are dearest to us?
> Do the stars listen, when we turn despairingly
> Away from man, or the great winds, or the seas or
> The mountains? To whom can any man say—Here I
> Am! Behold me in my nakedness, my wounds, my
> Secret grief, my despair, my betrayal, my pain,
> My tongue, which cannot express my sorrow, my
> Terror, my abandonment.
> Listen to me for a day—an hour! A moment!
> Lonely silence! O God, is there no one to listen?
> Is there no one to listen? you ask. Ah, yes,
> There is One who listens, who will always listen.
> Hasten to Him, my friend! He waits on the hill
> For you.

—Seneca

"Yes, there is One who listens, and many have learned to pour out their souls to God in earnest, satisfying prayer. But millions of others—perhaps the vast majority—are not so sure that He really listens and so do not seek the ear of this Listener. There is no verbal response from Him, no immediate sympathetic reply, and they doubt whether anyone is listening, after all."[7] Who listens to you in all the world or cares about the pain that wreaks havoc in your life?

Taylor Caldwell in *The Listener* says: "Man's real need, his most terrible need, is for someone to listen to him, not as a patient; but as a human soul."

June 28, 1976

Hi special people (Spiritual parents, Dean and Carole Benton)

I picked up your new album and book from Joan this morning. Have thought about you often lately and wish you were close enough to touch. I need to touch you. And then your voices walk into our home—fresh, real. I need you. I love you. I'm hurting. I hurt so bad. Does anyone care?

The world seems so superficial. I long for depth, for people to understand me—the depth of me. Who am I? I found myself and now I'm lost again. It hurts. Will I always be trying to discover who I am?

I don't like myself right now. I don't like what I'm doing to my family, especially Gary. I'm destroying his personhood. I'm robbing him of the joy of living. I keep begging his forgiveness and making new pledges to try to be a better person. But I can't seem to get off the merry-go-round, and I don't know where it's going or when it will stop.

---

[7] Cecil Osborne, *The Art of Understanding Yourself,* (Zondervan Books, January 1967)

Does any of this make sense? I'm confused. I hurt. I want to be vulnerable with someone, but I need them to be vulnerable with me, too. I need someone to listen to me. O God, is there no one to listen?

Marilyn

Then a cloud appeared and covered them, and a voice came from the cloud, "This is My Son, Whom I love. Listen to Him!" (Mark 9:7).

THE LISTENER

Do you hear the sound of silence in a world filled
    with noise?
Can you hear the One whose voice beckons you
    to listen to Him?
Or is silence ringing in your ears?
Life can be filled with the noise of the world.
It can subdue the solace our spirit yearns for.
It can bring anxiety that intrudes on the peace
    we seek.
Our Creator does not want the things of this
    world to drown out His voice.
His wish is that we will attune our ears to hear
    the sound of Him speaking.
His words can speak volumes to our hearts if we
    will but listen.
The Word says, "My sheep hear My voice."
Do you hear the voice of God speaking to you?
His voice can be thunderous in day or still at night.
The key to hearing is listening.
How can we be obedient to what He is saying if
    we do not listen?
How can we follow Him if we do not hear?
Sometimes God speaks to us in the whisper of a
    sunset.
Sometimes He calls us in the deep of our souls.
And sometimes His voice summons us in the
    chaos that surrounds us.

He can speak to us audibly or ever so softly in the innermost parts of our being.

Our hearts must cry out to reveal the hunger we are feeling.

Our thirst can only be quenched as we drink from the well of Living Water.

God, please speak to me. I desire to hear Your voice.

I desire to be filled from the provision of Your vast supply.

I desire to be your servant and fulfill Your will for my life.

You alone are my God, the Lover of my soul.

You alone are the One Who can speak grace to me.

You alone can minister to the depths of my soul.

I am listening, Father God.

Speak, I pray, so the world is drowned out from my hearing.

Speak, I pray, so that I can hear Your voice and follow You.

I am your servant, Lord.

You alone are the guardian of my soul.

Speak, and I will follow. Speak![8]

---

[8] Taylor Caldwell, *The Listener,* (Doubleday, 1960)

SILENCE

Come away with Me
by yourself to a quiet place
and get some rest.
(Mark 6:31)

Silence is the womb of all creation.[9]

Have you ever listened to silence? Have you sat in the midst of it and heard it calling your name? What is it saying to you? Is it berating you for something you have not done, perhaps not being obedient to the call deep within your soul? Or is it speaking inaudibly in a way that is seared into your memory bank, never to be silenced again?

Silence is not only the void of sound. You can hear it in a summer night's breeze, with crickets chirping in the glen. Or at daybreak when shafts of wheat sway quietly in the breeze. Or a babbling brook gently weaving its way downstream. You can see silence through a grove of trees, with the sun bursting forth to greet a new day or as it settles over God's creation at dusk. My spirit is calmed by the majestic beauty of Your creation, O Lord.

In *A Time for Everything*, Ecclesiastes 3:7b says, "There is a time to be silent and a time to speak." Speak, O silence, speak. What are you saying to me? What message are you trying to convey? I want to hear You. I don't want to shut out the stirrings deep within my soul. I long to accept the warmth of Your embrace. It soothes my spirit and fills me with peace. It brings solace to my heart and beckons me to come and sit in the quiet of Your presence.

---

[9] Deepak Chopra, *Why Is God Laughing?*, (Harmony, 2009)

Do not abandon me, breath of God. Do not forsake the longing of your servant. I need inspiration from on High. I need to know You are walking alongside me. I need to hear Your still, small voice in the bosom of my soul. "Hear, O Lord, and be merciful to me. O Lord, be my help" (Psalm 30:10).

I love You, O my God. I want to be obedient to your command. Your Word says You will not forsake me, but sometimes I feel so alone. I know full well that You indwell my very soul and long to quiet my spirit. I can hear You in my silence, but the sound of Your voice eludes me. I feel lonely and afraid. Please hear my cry. It is a cry for help and instruction. How am I able to be obedient to what I feel unable to achieve? I know your compassions fail not, but through my tears, the silence that envelops me is deafening.

I want to hear no other voice than Yours, dear Lord. Speak to my heart. Help me hear clearly how to answer the call You have placed on my life. Is it a figment of my imagination? Am I wasting Your time and mine? Am I rambling or do you hear the sound of my frustration? Sometimes it screams within me. I beat my chest, and the screaming prevails. My sleep is roused by bustling thoughts running rampant in my head.

I want my life to be fruitful and glorifying to You. You created me for a purpose. Your will is divine. You are Master. Please be Master of who I am and all You created me to be. I desire to be your lowly servant—to wipe my tears on the hem of Your garment—that I might be made whole and hold my head upright in Your Name.

Help me draw nigh unto You. Help me be faithful to the sound of Your voice in the silence of my heart. I so want to hear You, my Lord. With every fiber of my being, I long to be obedient. I surrender all that I am and ever hope to be. I am Yours, and You are mine. Receive my offering in the Name of Your Son, Jesus. To Him be all glory and honor and praise, both now and forevermore. Amen and amen!

I saw silence in the chapel at the Well of Mercy through a grove of trees, as the sun settled quietly over dusk's hush. I didn't have a camera to take a picture, but the sight of that silence is etched in my heart forever. God revealed Himself to me in a resounding, intimate way. He spoke into my stillness, "Your obedience does not come from asking to be obedient but, indeed, by being obedient." I heard more clear instructions than ever before. "Answer my call: write."

VICTORY

"Death has been swallowed up in victory."
"Where, O death, is your victory?"
"Where, O death, is your sting?"
"The sting of death is sin, and the power of sin
     is the law.
But thanks be to God!
He gives us the victory through our Lord Jesus
     Christ."
(1 Corinthians 15:54–57)

Are you experiencing victory in your life? Is victory a common thread that runs through the fabric of your being? Or is it fleeting and elusive to your everyday life? God meant for us to have, not only abundant life, but to live victoriously through Jesus Christ our Lord.

Do the doldrums often invade your spirit? Does your heart feel heavy, without the incentive to go forward with meaning and purpose for living? Have you ever been molested, not just sexually, but by thoughts that consume you mentally and emotionally? Does your spirit feel bruised from flagrant acts of injustice? Do you feel as if you have been raped by an evil presence over which you had no control?

In Psalm 20:4–5, David says, "May the Lord give you the desires of your heart and make all your plans succeed. We will shout for joy when you are victorious and will lift up our banners in the Name of our God. May the Lord grant all your requests."

Life can abruptly turn us into victims, but we have the power within to stave off that which would destroy us, leaving us injured and unable to live our lives in all its fullness. "The thief's purpose is to steal, kill, and destroy" (John 10:10). Jesus came that we might have life and have it abundantly.

Victory is not found in the ease of our circumstances nor in the strength of our own resources, but in the presence of the Lord Who is with us. Jesus is the difference, and He will make the difference in all we are going through.

God has made a way for our lives to be redeemed, making us victors rather than victims. His desire is that we fight off that which attacks us and leaves us bruised and battered by those who wish to harm us out of their anger or discontent. As Christians, we must rise from the garbage heap and move forward, so that our woundedness can become a healing agent for other souls that lie in ruins by life's destructive blows.

Sometimes we come into the world as babes—unwanted or not of the desired gender. Sometimes we don't even become aware of those things that make us feel unacceptable to mankind or the world at large until we've grown into adulthood. How do we overcome things that rob us of the very person God created us to be?

Psalm 139:14–16 says, "I praise You because I am fearfully and wonderfully made; Your works are wonderful, I know that full well. My frame was not hidden from You when I was made in the secret place, when I was woven together in the depths of the earth, Your eyes saw my unformed body. All the days ordained for me were written in Your book before one of them came to be."

In Luke 10:19, Jesus tells us, "I have given you authority to trample on snakes and scorpions and to overcome all the power of the enemy; nothing will harm you." What power has been bestowed on us, if we will but take hold of it. God's Word is truth, and we must abide by it. Ask! Believe! Receive!

We can indeed be attacked by a myriad of evil things in this wretched world. But God has given us the power to rise up from the ashes that burn within our souls and overcome in the Name of Jesus. We don't have the power within ourselves to resist that which seeks to overcome us, but the One who sacrificed His life for us stands ready to fight our battles and make us victors over the wiles of the one who came to steal, kill, and destroy.

What joy is ours when we fight the good fight and become victorious over that which would devour our molested, wounded souls. Our Lord Himself was beaten beyond recognition. He willingly laid down His life that we might rise from that which seeks to make us victims rather than victors. We can overcome by the blood of the Lamb and by the word of our testimony (Revelation 12:11a).

God does desire that we live victoriously. Sometimes we can get bogged down in the tragedies of yesterday and the trials that are besetting us on every side, along with fears that might await us on the horizon.

Faith in our Lord is the key for our future. He holds us in the palms of His hands, and we can be assured that He is trustworthy. "This is the victory that has overcome the world, even our faith. Who is it that overcomes the world? Only he who believes that Jesus is the Son of God" (1 John 5:4–5). We can't experience victory unless we are willing to open ourselves to overcoming that which hinders us from living the victorious life.

"For I know the plans I have for you," declares the Lord, "plans to prosper you and not to harm you, plans to give you hope and a future. Then you will call upon Me and come and pray to Me, and I will listen to you. You will seek Me and find Me when you seek Me with all your heart" (Jeremiah 29:11–13).

Are you seeking the Lord with all your heart? What is hindering you from trusting Him and His plans for your future? His Word tells us He is good. He desires the very best for us—beyond our wildest hopes and imaginings. We will not be able to overcome if we do not keep our eyes on Him and seek Him with all our heart. Psalm 60:12a says, "With God we will gain the victory!"

A Vince Lombardi quote states, "I firmly believe that any man's finest hour, the greatest fulfillment of all that he holds dear, is that moment when he has worked his heart out in a good cause and lies exhausted on the field of battle—victorious."

The stone has been rolled away.
Arise!
Our Savior lives!

CONFESS, COMMUNE, COMMIT

I was sitting in the parking lot of Union Baptist Church in Leicester, North Carolina, looking over a valley, overlooking a mountain with ridge tops on the horizon partially covered by fog that lifted as I sought the Lord for the anguish that had taken up residence in my soul.

After spending several minutes in tears, I said to Father God, "I have no words. I need You to speak. I need to hear from You." In my spirit, I then asked the Lord to please lift the fog that partially covered me.

I want to see you clearly and again ask You to reveal Yourself to me, and then what You would have me do with my life. I so much want everything I do and say to bring glory and honor to Who You are—to Your presence in my life. We both know that everything I do and say does not. The tears in my eyes and the cry of my heart is because I have once again fallen short of Your glory and hurt my beloved husband Gary by the wake of my torrential, disparaging words.

I long to sit in Your Presence and be renewed and restored by Your Holy Spirit. I invite You to be my Counselor. Please guard my heart so that what comes out of my mouth—that has been bred in my heart—will bring edification to my beloved Gary and glorification to You, the Lover of my soul.

My heart sings praises for Your unconditional love and mercy. As this Baptist church sings its praises to You and Gary worships You in spirit and truth at Crossroads' early service, I pray that I will be filled with a wellspring of joy and gladness. The prayer of my heart is that Your Light will radiate in and through me to all I encounter along Your path for my life.

In preparation for Communion this morning, Father God, I desire nothing more than to commune with You in my spirit and in truth. I don't want to go to Your house and feel like I have to wear a mask. Help me feel the freedom to be who I am this day.

Your creation is full of bountiful richness. Your pastures are lush with Your nature. Help my life to be lush with Your nature, dear Jesus. Wash my heart with Your shed blood. I wish You hadn't had to die for me and my sin, but I, too, am a sinner in need of Your grace.

"Father, forgive me for falling short again. Cleanse me of all, all, all my unrighteousness. Take the bitter gall in my heart that spews out of my mouth and crucify it in Your precious Holy Name. All I can offer You this morning is bitterness and strife. Please, please make something beautiful of my life. I am helpless without You, Jesus."

"May the God of hope fill me with all joy and peace as I trust in You, so that I may overflow with hope by the power of Your Holy Spirit" (Romans 15:13).

Once again, dear Jesus, I commit my life to You. May my journey through this valley bring me to new heights with You.

In Your Name and for Your glory,
Marilyn

Sunday, August 24, 2003
Three days before my sixtieth birthday

JESUS' INVITATIONS

I asked Jesus to live in my heart on November 8, 1972. It is the most wonderful thing I will ever do!

A catalyst God used to call me to bend my knee and bow my heart as I invited His one and only Son, Jesus, into my heart was written by Bill Bright of Campus Crusade for Christ. Along with this salvation tract, I feel led to share several other tracts that might bring you to accept Jesus' invitation. It is my prayer that God's Holy Spirit will speak to your heart and spirit as you come to know Jesus as your personal Savior and Lord. There is nothing more important you can do on this earth than ask Jesus into your heart and life! May you be blessed as you walk forth in His Name for His glory. So be it, Lord Jesus.

HAVE YOU HEARD OF THE FOUR SPIRITUAL LAWS?

Just as there are physical laws that govern the physical universe, so there are spiritual laws that govern your relationship with God.

Law 1: God loves you and offers a wonderful plan for your life.

God's Love: "God so loved the world that He gave His one and only Son, that whoever believes in Him shall not perish but have eternal life" (John 3:16, NIV).

God's Plan: [Christ speaking] "I came that they might have life, and might have it abundantly" [that it might be full and meaningful] (John 10:10).

Why is it that most people are not experiencing the abundant life?

Because...

Law 2: Man is sinful and separated from God. Therefore, he cannot know and experience God's love and plan for his life.

Man Is Sinful: "All have sinned and fall short of the glory of God" (Romans 3:23).

Man was created to have fellowship with God; but, because of his own stubborn self-will, he chose to go his own independent way and fellowship with God was broken. This self-will, characterized by an attitude of active rebellion or passive indifference, is an evidence of what the Bible calls sin.

Man Is Separated: "The wages of sin is death" [spiritual separation from God] (Romans 6: 23).

Holy God: God is holy, and man is sinful. A great gulf separates the two. Man is continually trying to reach God and the abundant life through his own efforts, such as a good life, philosophy, or religion—but he inevitably fails.

Sinful Man: The third law explains the only way to bridge this gulf…

Law 3: Jesus Christ is God's only provision for man's sin. Through Him you can know and experience God's love and plan for your life.

He Died In Our Place: "God demonstrates His own love toward us, in that while we were yet sinners, Christ died for us" (Romans 5:8).

He Rose From The Dead: "Christ died for our sins… He was buried… He was raised on the third day, according to the Scriptures… He appeared to Peter, then to the twelve. After that He appeared to more than five hundred" (1 Corinthians 15:3–6).

He Is The Only Way To God: "Jesus said to him, 'I am the way, and the truth, and the life; no one comes to the Father but through Me'" (John 14:6).

God—God has bridged the gulf that separates us from Him by sending His Son,

Jesus—Jesus Christ, to die on the cross in our place to pay the penalty for our sins.

Man—It is not enough just to know these three laws…

Law 4: We must individually receive Jesus Christ as Savior and Lord; then we can know and experience God's love and plan for our lives.

We Must Receive Christ: "As many as received Him, to them He gave the right to become children of God, even to those who believe in His Name" (John 1:12).

We Receive Christ Through Faith: "By grace you have been saved through faith; and that not of yourselves, it is the gift of God; not as a result of works that no one should boast" (Ephesians 2:8–9).

When We Receive Christ, We Experience A New Birth: (Read John 3:1–8.)

We Receive Christ Through Personal Invitation: [Christ speaking] "Behold, I stand at the door and knock; if anyone hears My voice and opens the door, I will come in to him" (Revelation 3:20).

Receiving Christ involves turning to God from self (repentance) and trusting Christ to come into our lives to forgive our sins and make us what He wants us to be. Just to agree intellectually that Jesus Christ is the Son of God and that He died on the cross for our sins is not enough. Nor is it enough to have an emotional experience. We receive Jesus Christ by faith, as an act of the will.

The following represent two kinds of lives:

Self-Directed Life
S Self is on the throne
+ Christ is outside the life
- Interests are directed by self, often resulting in discord and frustration.

Christ-Directed Life
+ Christ is in the life and on the throne
S Self is yielding to Christ
- Interests are directed by Christ, resulting in harmony with God's plan.

Which best represents your life?

Which would you like to have represent your life?

The following explains how you can receive Christ:

You Can Receive Christ Right Now By Faith Through Prayer (Prayer is talking with God.)
God knows your heart and is not so concerned with your words as He is with the attitude of your heart. The following is a suggested prayer:

"Lord Jesus, I need You. Thank you for dying on the cross for my sins. I open the door of my life and receive You as my Savior and Lord. Thank You for forgiving my sins and giving me eternal life.

Take control of the throne of my life. Make me the kind of person You want me to be."

Does this prayer express the desire of our heart?

If it does, I invite you to pray this prayer right now, and Christ will come into your life, as He promised.

How To Know That Christ Is In Your Life

Did you receive Christ into your life? According to His promise in Revelation 3:20, where is Christ right now in relation to you? Christ said that He would come into your life. Would He mislead you? On what authority do you know that God has answered your prayer? (The trustworthiness of God Himself and His Word.)

The Bible Promises Eternal Life to All Who Receive Christ

"The witness is this, that God has given us eternal life, and this life is in His Son. He who has the Son has the life; he who does not have the Son of God does not have the life. These things I have written to you who believe in the Name of the Son of God, in order that you may know that you have eternal life" (1 John 5:11–13).

Thank God often that Christ is in your life and that He will never leave you (Hebrews 13:5). You can know on the basis of His promise that Christ lives in you and that you have eternal life from the very moment you invite Him in. He will not deceive you.

An important reminder... **Do Not Depend on Feelings**

The promise of God's Word, the Bible—not our feelings—is our authority. The Christian lives by faith (trust) in the trustworthiness of God Himself and His Word. A train illustrates the relationship among **fact** (God and His Word), **faith** (our trust in God and His Word), and **feeling** (the result of our faith and obedience). (Read John 14:21.)

A train will run with or without the caboose. However, it would be useless to attempt to pull a train by the caboose. In the same way, as Christians, we do not depend on feelings or emotions, but we place our faith (trust) in the trustworthiness of God and the promises of His Word.

Now That You Have Received Christ

The moment you received Christ by faith, as an act of the will, many things happened, including the following:

- Christ came into your life (Revelation 3:20; Colossians 1:27).
- Your sins were forgiven (Colossians 1:14).
- You became a child of God (John 1:12).
- You received eternal life (John 5:24).
- You began the great adventure for which God created you (John 10:10; 2 Corinthians 5:17; 1 Thessalonians 5:18).

Can you think of anything more wonderful that could happen to you than receiving Christ? Would you like to thank God in prayer right now for what He has done for you? By thanking God, you demonstrate your faith.

Suggestions for Christian Growth

Spiritual growth results from trusting Jesus Christ. "The righteous man shall live by faith" (Galatians 3:11). A life of faith will enable you to trust God increasingly with every detail of your life, and to practice the following:

G: *Go* to God in prayer daily (John 15:7).

R: *Read* God's Word daily (Acts 17:11); begin with the Gospel of John.

O: *Obey* God moment by moment (John 14:21).

W: *Witness* for Christ by your life and words (Matthew 4:19; John 15:8).

T: *Trust* God for every detail of your life (1 Peter 5:7).

H: *Holy Spirit*—allow Him to control and empower your daily life and witness (Galatians 5:16–17; Acts 1:8).

137

Fellowship in a Good Church

God's Word instructs us not to forsake "the assembling of ourselves together" (Hebrews 10:25). Several logs burn brightly together, but put one aside on the cold hearth and the fire goes out. So it is with your relationship with other Christians.

If you do not belong to a church, do not wait to be invited. Take the initiative; call the pastor of a nearby church where Christ is honored and His Word is preached. Start this week and make plans to attend regularly.

Special Materials Are Available for Christian Growth

If you have come to know Christ personally through this presentation of the gospel, helpful materials for Christian growth are available to you. For more information, write Campus Crusade for Christ, 100 Sunport Lane 2100, Orlando, FL 32809.

If this booklet has been helpful to you, please share it with someone else.[10]

> NewLife Publications
> A Ministry of Campus Crusade for Christ
> Copyright Permission Granted

---

[10] Bill Bright, *Have You Heard of the Four Spiritual Laws?*, 1965–2018, The Bright Media Foundation and Campus Crusade for Christ, Inc. All rights reserved, http://crustor.org/four-spiritual-laws-online/ Included by permission.

THE SALVATION POEM

Jesus, You died upon a cross
Romans 5:8

And rose again to save the lost
John 3:16

Forgive me now of all my sin
1 John 1:9

Come be my Savior, Lord, and Friend
Romans 10:9

Change my life and make it new
2 Corinthians 5:17

And help me, Lord, to live for You
Colossians 2:6

Today I have received Jesus Christ as the Savior and Lord of my life.

Signature _____ Date _____

The Billy Graham Library

CELEBRATE

"I tell you the truth, today you will be with Me in paradise" (Luke 23:43).

Because Jesus Christ
Died and rose again,
You can have new life.

"For God so loved the world that He gave His One and only Son, that whoever believes in Him shall not perish but have eternal life." (John 3:16)

As Jesus hung on the cross, the last person He spoke to was a prisoner who was being executed alongside Him. Even while suffering in horrible pain, Jesus cared enough to forgive the man and promise him a place in Heaven.

Jesus wants to do the same for you. Ask Him to forgive your sins and become the Lord of your life. You can have peace with God and the assurance of a new life now and forever.

I'm praying that the love of Jesus Christ will touch you and your family. May you find new life in Him.

A friend who cares,
Marilyn

"Whoever hears My word and believes Him who sent Me has eternal life and will not be condemned; he has crossed over from death to life."

The Words Of Jesus Recorded In John 5:24

Jesus loves *you*
this I know
For the Bible
tells me so.

Jesus will never stop loving *you*.
Whether you're happy, sad, scared,
or lonely… He's promised to love
and take care of *you*.

From a friend who is praying for you!
Marilyn

May God add His blessing to these Salvation Plans as He uses His Holy Spirit to draw you unto Him.

EPILOGUE

Wounded Soldiers Marching toward Victory

I have experienced pain in my life, and my heart hurts for the pain in yours, fellow sojourner. Father God is in the process of making my pain *broken unto wholeness*, and my prayer for you is that you are at the place in your life where you can allow Him to bring you into wholeness, as well.

His Word tells us that "The Lord is close to the brokenhearted and saves those who are crushed in spirit" (Psalm 34:18), and "He heals the brokenhearted and binds up their wounds" (Psalm 147:3).

Will you allow the Lord to heal your broken heart and bind up your wounds? He came to set you free from the things that hold you captive. Come out of your prison without bars. Jesus is waiting to set you free, dear one. Give Him permission to make the word of your testimony: "Whom the Lord has set free, is free indeed" (John 8:36). He is our cheerleader waiting at the finish line to utter, "Well done, good and faithful servant."

I want to thank you for sharing my book and part of my journey with me. I pray your life has been enriched, as you have enriched mine by your willingness to jog down this path of my life.

If you have wounds in your life that haven't healed because they are infected with self-hatred or feelings of abandonment, rejection, or whatever your case may be—seek the only true source for your healing. Let the shed blood of Jesus wash over you, and let Him pour the balm of Gilead over all the places in your spirit that cry out in pain. He is the Healer, and He desires to make you...

Broken unto Wholeness.

This is not my final chapter!

Glory be unto the Father, and to the Son, and to the Holy Spirit: as it was in the beginning, is now, and ever shall be, world without end. Amen.

Lightning Source UK Ltd.
Milton Keynes UK
UKHW011245130720
366458UK00002B/416